# What Are You Doing for Lunch?

## MONA MEIGHAN Ed.D.

Contributing Author SARA DEHART MSN, Ph.D.

BOOK PUBLISHERS NETWORK

Book Publishers Network
P. O. Box 2256
Bothell, WA 98041
425-483-3040
www.bookpublishersnetwork.com

10 9 8 7 6 5 4 3 2 1

LCCN:  2012935529
ISBN 13:  978-1-937454-30-2

**Authors' Note:**
Although the information is believed to be accurate at the time of going to press, neither the authors nor the publisher can accept any legal responsibility for omissions, cost differentiation, general or nutritional value errors nor from any harm that may come from following the instructions in this book.

Book design and layout: Asha Hossain Design, Inc. • www.ashahossain.com
Editor: Jill Kelly, Ph.D.

# A Tribute to My Son Luke

 This book is dedicated to my son Luke, who died in 2009 at the age of 26. Luke was not known for his love of healthy food, but he did love to eat. For the seven years before his death, while he was in college and then working, his choices primarily consisted of pizza, fast food, pop, and sweet desserts. All of the speeches from loved ones could not change his eating habits.

When we received the call that Luke had died with no apparent cause, we were determined to figure out the cause. After waiting a very long eight weeks for a full autopsy, we learned that he had died from a type of diabetes. With no diabetes history in his family and even though he had had three normal glucose readings in the previous five years, we learned that diabetes could still take a young person's life.

I wrote this book to help young adults and their families recognize the importance of paying attention to what they eat. While we should pay attention to all the food consumed during the day, *What Are You Doing for Lunch?* concentrates on a meal often sacrificed. Besides the importance of eating healthier food and knowing the ingredients of the food you are eating, this book also focuses on how much money you can save by taking 15 to 20 minutes a day to prepare a lunch. For instance, if you make one lunch a week instead of eating in a restaurant, do you know how much you can save in one month, in one year?

A portion of the proceeds from this book is being donated to non-profit organizations in honor of Luke and to support the enlightened awareness of healthier and economical lunches for all.

# Table of Contents

Recipes at a Glance, Ingredients and a Grab and Go List are available at
www.whatareyoudoingforlunch.com

# List of Recipes

## Soups

Grandma's Chicken Soup
Fresh Vegetable Soup
Tomato and Basil Soup
Chicken Tortilla Soup
Vegetarian Corn Chowder
Vegetarian Minestrone Soup
Fresh Carrot Soup

## Salads

Basil, Tomato, and Mozzarella Cheese Salad
Smoked Salmon and Greens
Tuna Avocado Salad
Spinach Salad with Feta and Walnuts
Strawberry/Mango Salad
Classic Caesar Salad
Mixed Green Salad
Fruit and Nut Salad
Black Bean and Corn Salad
Fresh Salmon and Spinach Salad
Pasta Salad with Black Beans and Spinach
Fresh Fruit Salad
Greek Tofu Salad
Egg Salad with Apples and Almonds

## Main Course Entrées

Homemade Vegetable Stew
Easy Spinach Lasagna
Cooking a Whole Chicken
Homemade Chili
Homemade Vegetarian Chili
Homemade Meatballs
Beef and Tomato Stew
Roast Beef for Sandwiches

# About the Book

My research shows that going to an average restaurant costs at least $10-$15 per person when the tip is added into the bill. While it is true that that you can go to a fast-food restaurant for less money, the recipes in this book are usually not found in these restaurants.

Prices change by location and season, but most recipes in this book cost about 1/3 of what you would pay for an equivalent meal in a restaurant. Another advantage of brown bagging is that you know the ingredients that you put into a recipe; often this is not clear when you buy a restaurant meal.

I encourage you to use fresh ingredients. None of the recipes require the use of a microwave oven. While it is okay to use a microwave oven occasionally, some nutritionists are urging caution in the daily use of these ovens to cook meals. A small hot plate can be used to heat soups at the office.

Before starting on *What Are You Doing for Lunch?* take the Personal Lunch Style Assessment found on page 5. If you come out as a Grab and Go lunch person, try to expand the list found on page 18 with your favorites. Having a food item on the list will ensure that you buy the items the next time you food shop rather than buying lunch from the office vending machine. A Grab and Go person may want to try some recipes, but just getting into the habit of weekly food shopping and purchasing enough healthy items, you likely will save money and improve the nutritional value of your lunches.

# Why These Recipes?

The recipes were chosen for a number of reasons. First, these dishes are ones that many people like and may order in a restaurant; second, they are easy to make and the cost of the ingredients in most of the recipes is comparatively low.

Most of the recipes take no longer than 20 minutes to create though some of the soups and entrée meals take longer to cook on the stove or in the oven, but your preparation time is still about 15-20 minutes. If you do not have too much experience with recipes, these are easy to follow and understand. All of the ingredients are found in grocery stores, and a list of kitchen tools and pantry items can be found on pages 8 and 9.

Many of the recipes are vegetarian, but if you prefer, you can add meat to any of the salads. If you are calculating your savings, always remember to add ingredients into the total cost of a recipe. To find all the Vegetarian lunches, go to Recipes at a Glance on page 113. Once you have established a month of lunches, you may just want to repeat the lunches you especially liked and add some new ones for month two. This change in your lunch patterns may stimulate a new interest for you to attempt other recipes. More recipes can be found on the websites listed on page 120.

## How to Carry Your Lunch

One decision you will need to make is what you are going to put your lunch in and what carriers and utensils you will use. There are always the traditional plastic bags and disposable containers and you can go online (see page 121) to find lots of fun, stylish lunch products that are not disposable. Before making your decision as to what to use, you may want to read lunch waste data on www.worldcentric. org. I hope this book will not only encourage you to begin a healthier lunch habit, but also help you to become aware of the importance of using non-disposable products.

## Enjoy the Challenge

Enjoy the challenge of creating new healthier habits at lunch. Please let me know how you are doing by visiting my website: www.whatareyoudoingforlunch.com

—Mona Meighan

# Acknowledgements

When I began thinking of this book, I knew I would need a supportive community or "village" of friends and professionals to help me complete it.

I am beyond grateful to my niece who was with me on this project from Day 1. Her supportive love, ideas, and editing skills helped me take one task at a time and not give up.

Others in my community included my children who gave me honest feedback, especially when I really didn't want it. At the same time, they created a mantra when my focus began to stray of "Mom, just finish the book."

My partner Kelly listened and was there for me throughout the process, but I sometimes had the feeling he wondered what I was doing for two and a half years. His loving support kept me going at my own pace.

A big thanks to Serena Sconzo. who dedicated many hours of her summer vacation to help enter data and taste some of the recipes.

I was so delighted to recruit my contributing author and friend Dr. Sara Dehart. Her expertise in nutrition and her ability to describe the health benefits of each recipe were invaluable, but even more important was the nurturing feedback she provided throughout the process.

When I visited my dear friend John Lewis in Berkeley 2 years ago, he gave me so much courage to undergo this endeavor and convinced me to calculate the cost of each recipe and show savings over a period of time. Sorry you are not here to see the book in print. R.I.P.

Dan Myers, a professional photographer and childhood friend of my son, Luke, took my bio photo. We met at Luke's memorial bench early one morning, and when he completed the shoot, he told me he was honored to provide the picture in memory of Luke and refused to accept money. My professional team of Asha Hossain, graphic designer, and editors Christa Gardner and Jill Kelly, PhD, were so competent and patient with me while bringing life to my first book.

There are so many others I can't begin to list, who gave me crucial feedback on the recipes and praise for what I was doing, knowing the book was helping to keep me grounded and sane while going through the grieving process.

# What You Eat for Lunch Does Matter

In May, 2011, a full-page advertisement appeared in newspapers across the country that was signed or endorsed by more than 1,750 health professionals and their institutions. Their ad, addressed to McDonald's CEO, Jim Skinner, pleaded with him to stop targeting our kids with his fast food, and junk food advertising and promotions.[1]

One in three American children is at risk for developing type 2 diabetes at some point in their life. This is the cumulative result of lifelong habits, learned early. We are teaching our children to seek satisfaction on many levels, by stuffing themselves with manufactured products high in fat and corn syrup sweeteners. As a result, experts warn that this generation may be the first in U.S. history to live shorter lives than their parents.

Commercial marketing has changed the way American youth eat, by changing our expectations and our automatic responses to stimuli, like hunger.

So-called "fast foods" now feature prominently in many school lunch programs. The official rationale is that such "empty calorie" products are the only foods that kids will eat. But is this true? Does it have to be this way, or can we wean them from a lifelong addiction to a suicide diet, and lead them back to healthier, lifelong eating habits? You can examine more statistics by visiting the fastfoodmarketing. org website.

## Does it have to be this way?

I believe that there is an alternative to commercial fast food lunches, and *What Are You Doing for Lunch?* is my answer.

Perhaps you are a concerned parent picking up this book to send a tangible message to your son or daughter or even a grandchild. Perhaps you are a consumer trying to save some money by not putting your extra cash into some restaurant or fast food establishment. No matter what your circumstances, this

[1] Lynn, P. (June 20, 2011). McDiabetes; Top Docs Tell McDonald's to Stop Marketing Junk. Institute for Policy Studies (IPS).

book is an offering to help you discover real food again, and help nurture your body back into balance and health.

Brown bagging our lunches and our children's lunches may be one major way to help kids survive in this era of commercial marketing.

I wrote *What Are You Doing for Lunch?* to help people who want to change their lunch habits do this by eating healthier foods, saving money, and enjoying the nourishment food brings on many levels. How to change our attitude about lunch is a one-step-at-a-time transformation.

• Become aware of your lunch style and ask yourself if your body really likes what you've just eaten.

• After eating a meal of empty calories ask: Does my body really like what I've just eaten?

• Changing lunch habits and staying with it is like beginning and sticking with an exercise program.

• Once you learn some basics, use some of the easy recipes or just use the Grab and Go list to help you get started.

• The recipes are easy to make and none take longer than 20 minutes to prepare.

## Habits Are Our Default System

Both good and bad habits take about 30 days to develop so give yourself time to feel comfortable with new eating patterns. If you can convince a friend or co-worker to join you in this new endeavor, your chances of changing what you are doing for lunch is greater than if you do it alone. We all need support to make a change.

# Have You Thought About the Benefits of Brown Bagging?

The main reason most people eat out rather than bring their own lunch to work or school is time. And it's true. Brown bagging does take a little time. But with this book, the emphasis is on little: you can make every recipe in 20 minutes or less.

And once you recognize the benefits of brown bagging, like saving money, improving your health, and actually getting more time and flexibility in your day, you'll see how a little effort leads to big rewards.

## You can save money.

- Create an entire week of healthy lunches for the same price as eating in a restaurant just once.

- Spend $5.00 or less on each recipe, a $1.50-$5.00 savings compared to buying a similar item in a restaurant.

- Look to the long term with one-month and one-year cost-savings projections for each recipe.

**Food for Thought:**
Donate the money you save to a cause close to your heart.

## You can improve your health.

- Know exactly what you're eating and have more control over quality, calories, fat, salt, and sugar.

- Easily make meals vegetarian or adjust cheese, condiments, and seasoning to your tastes.

- Take a walk or hit the gym instead of spending your lunch hour standing in line or sitting in a noisy restaurant.

> **Food for Thought:**
> Support the health of the planet by using a re-usable bag and washable containers.

## You can enjoy convenience and flexibility.

- Eat lunch where and with whom you want.

- After lunch, run errands, pay bills, or take care of other tasks that make your life easier at the end of the day.

- Stay active with hobbies and interests by taking 20 minutes to do what you love or to learn something new on your lunch break.

> **Food for Thought:**
> Volunteer at a local soup kitchen on your lunch hour.

- Create a brown-bagging buddy system with a friend or co-worker for support.

- Be a model for healthy eating and make a homemade snack to share with your class or office mates.

- Bring restaurant finesse to brown bagging by planning family-style shared lunches with friends.

> **Food for Thought:**
> Double your recipe and bring lunch for a friend or colleague you know could use it, or a person in need out on the street.

# What Is Your Personal Lunch Style?

This book contains recipes to accommodate five lunch styles. Depending on your lifestyle and what you want to accomplish by reading this book, you can probably tell what category is closest to your style. Remember, lunch styles can also vary by the day depending on how much time you have to spend on creating your lunch. The following chart helps determine your lunch style.

By completing the 10 questions below, you can tell what section(s) of the book you want to begin in. Remember, changing your old lunch habits is the goal, so feel free to use any section of the book that will help you accomplish it. Think of adding items from the Grab and Go list to round out your lunch.

| Question | Answer | Lunch Style Recipes | Page |
|---|---|---|---|
| 1. Do you want to save money on your lunches? | If YES: | You probably will sustain some change in your lunch pattern. | 17 |
| 2. Do you want to eat healthier foods for lunch? | If YES: | Go to the Grab and Go and Almost Grab and Go lunch style pages of the book. | 17 |
| 3. Are you willing to spend approximately 30 minutes a week before you go to the grocery store to plan lunch ideas? | If YES: | Go to the Grab and Go and Almost Grab and Go lunch style pages of the book. | 17 |
| 4. Do you find yourself making the same lunches day after day? | If YES: | Go to the Traditionalist lunch style pages and review previous sections of the book. | 31 |
| 5. Are you interested in ways to vary your traditional lunches? | If YES: | Go to the Traditionalist lunch style pages and review Grab and Go and Almost Grab and Go sections of the book. | 31 |

| Question | Answer | Lunch Style Recipes | Page |
|---|---|---|---|
| 6. Are you willing to spend approximately 15-20 minutes either in the evening or in the morning preparing your lunch? | If YES: | Go to the Creative lunch style pages and review previous sections of the book. | 43 |
| 7. Are you willing to spend time on the weekends or in the evening preparing food for the week's lunches? | If YES: | Go to the Midday Gourmet lunch style pages and review previous sections of the book. | 65 |
| 8. Are you willing to stock your kitchen with the common ingredients and tools needed for easy lunch preparation? | If YES: | Go to the Midday Gourmet lunch style pages and review previous sections of the book. | 65 |
| 9. Are you interested in sharing lunches with others at work or school? | If YES: | Go to the Social Networker lunch style pages and review previous sections of the book, | 99 |
| 10. Are you interested in creating five lunches once a week and sharing this process with four friends who are also willing to do it? | If YES: | Go to the Social Networker lunch style pages and review previous sections of the book, | 99 |

## Reminders

1. If you are using this book solely for economic reasons, make sure you include similar ingredients for several days of the week. This will cut down on waste because of food spoilage.

2. If brown bagging your lunch is new to you, start slowly, maybe just once or twice a week, and then gradually increase the days.

3. If you find yourself getting discouraged, give yourself a break and set a time when you will begin bringing your lunch again.

4. Make this book your own. Jot down notes on the recipe pages.

# Organizing Your Kitchen for Lunches

Before you begin preparing your healthier lunches, you need to make sure you have the necessary kitchen tools to make the job easier. Many cookbooks have long lists of kitchen items needed in the pantry and cupboards, but since this book is about creating easy recipes and saving money on lunches, I've included only items that will make your lunch preparation easier. Always feel free to modify the list and create other easy ways of preparing the food.

I also suggest buying the staple ingredients when you are planning to make a recipe that calls for them and remember to look for other recipes that use the leftovers or same ingredients. This will definitely save you money.

Tools for the kitchen include pots and pans, knives and silverware, kitchen accessories and storage containers, that double for leftovers and bringing your soups and salads to lunch.

Before you start, think of what you will be putting your lunch in to pack and carry, including items that are disposable and recyclable. I think we all know the benefits of choosing recyclable containers, but I trust you to choose what will help you make a more healthful lunch more often. If you are interested in seeing many options for storage containers and lunch bags, see the websites listed on page 121.

Following is a list of all the kitchen tools and pantry items used in the book.

# Kitchen Tools

## Pots, Pans, and Appliances

1 small pot with lid (approx. 1.5 qt.)

1 medium pot with lid (approx .3 qt.)

1 large pot with lid (approx .5 qt.)

1 Dutch oven (6 qt. pot with lid) or crockpot

12-cup muffin baking pan

Baking or cookie sheet

Baking pan (approx. 18x12x2) (You can use aluminum foil for a cover if it doesn't come with one)

Blender, food processor, or juicer

Casserole pan

Large frying pan (9 in.)

## Knives and Silverware

3-4 in. paring knife

7-8 in. butcher knife

Table knife for spreads and cutting sandwiches

Vegetable peeler

At least 2 forks, spoons, and knives (could be plastic or disposable) for eating

## Accessories

Small mixing bowl (approx. 7 in.)

Medium mixing bowl (approx. 8 in.)

Large mixing bowl (approx. 9 in.)

Can opener

Cheese grater

Cutting board (8x6 should be large enough or your choice)

Egg beater/whisk

Measuring cups (1 cup, 1/2 cup, 1/3 cup, 1/4 cup)

Measuring spoons (1 tablespoon, 1 teaspoon, 1/2 teaspoon, 1/4 teaspoon)

Mixing spoons and forks for mixing and mashing

Strainer

## Storage Containers

Medium and large plastic or glass storage containers to store leftovers and to carry your lunch in

Large serving platter, bowls, and serving spoons for Social Network lunches

## Pantry Items

*Common items that need refrigeration after purchase and opening.*

Butter or margarine

Dijon mustard and regular mustard

Eggs

Garlic cloves

Jam/jelly

Lemon juice

Mayonnaise

Olives

Parmesan cheese

Peanut butter

Salad dressing (favorite and balsamic oil and vinegar)

Canned Goods

Chicken broth and vegetable broth

Corn (whole kernel and creamed)
Diced tomatoes
Garbanzo beans (chickpeas)
Kidney beans
Pasta, spaghetti, or marinara sauce
Stewed tomatoes
Water-packed tuna
Tomato sauce

## Baking
All purpose flour
Baking powder
Brown sugar
Cooking spray
Honey or agave nectar
Sugar
Whole-wheat flour

## Oils and Vinegars
Canola oil
Olive oil
Vegetable oil
Balsamic vinegar
White wine vinegar

## Dried Goods and Nuts
Almonds
Breadcrumbs
Raisins
Walnuts

## Herbs and Spices
Chili powder
Curry powder
Garlic powder and salt
Ground cinnamon
Oregano or Italian seasoning
Pepper
salt (preferably sea salt)
Chicken and vegetable broth, granules
  or cubes

## Pastas
Lasagna
Macaroni
Penne

## Miscellaneous
Aluminum foil
Paper muffin cup liners, if making
  nutritional muffins
Paper bags – if not using recyclable
  bags for carrying lunch
Paper towels
Plastic storage bags
Plastic wrap
Sandwich bags – if not using recyclable
  bags
Toothpicks

# 8 Steps to Planning a Week of Lunches

Everyone can succeed with this 8-step process. As Nike says, Just Do It!

**Step 1. Determine your lunch style.**
Complete the questions on the Personal Lunch Style chart found on page 5. Begin your healthful lunch savings journey with the style that most fits you right now.

I began as a Creative Lunch but always had a day or two of Grab and Go lunches.

**Step 2. Determine how many lunches you need to bring next week.**
Look at your calendar and see how many days you need to bring your lunch. Depending on your schedule, you may be involved with lunch meetings, going out for a birthday celebration, etc.

I know that next week there are only 3 days I need to brown bag. If you are used to eating out 5 days a week, you may want to continue eating out some but determine the number of lunches you need to plan for.

**Step 3. Determine your weekly recipes.**
Look at the recipes in the section of your personal lunch style and choose the recipes that look good. Key in on how much you will be saving, how good the recipe sounds, and how easy the recipe is to create.

It's fine to browse other sections, but start small so you don't get discouraged. And it's okay to have 5 Grab and Go days. Write your choices on the monthly calendar found on page 110.

**Step 4. Determine the ingredients, kitchen tools, and pantry items needed.**
If using your kitchen is a new adventure and you don't have the kitchen tools or pantry items, ask friends if they have some to share, or go to a thrift shop or merchandise store. Most grocery stores have basic tools, but you will get better choices and sometimes cheaper prices at stores where there is a kitchen section. Record the ingredients needed from your recipe and check your pantry items.

### Step 5. Create a shopping list.

A sample shopping list form is found on page 111 or use a blank piece of paper. Record on your shopping list the ingredients you do not have in your kitchen.

I enjoy using the form provided here because it saves me time in the food store when all of the items in the same category are together on my list.

### Step 6. Go food shopping.

Try to stick to your list, but remember you may want to add some Grab and Go items to round out your lunch. Remember to calculate these items on the total cost of lunch. If there are favorite things you found and want to remember them, add the items to your Grab and Go list  on page 112.

### Step 7. Calculate the costs of your lunches.

Each recipe lists the cost of food or you can get your prices from Recipes at a Glance found on page 113. Add the cost of the additional items you included on your grocery list to determine the total cost of your lunch. Record that on the monthly calendar. For example, remember to calculate a portion of the price of a large bag of popcorn if you ate only a portion of it. It is most economical to either repeat lunches or use similar ingredients during the week to avoid food waste as much as possible.

### Step 8. Determine savings.

Look at either the recipe or Recipes at a Glance on page 113 and calculate how much the recipe you made would have cost in a restaurant. Record that figure on the monthly calendar found on page 110. Pay attention to the figures of how much you can save in one month, and one year if you make this lunch just once a week. If you are serious about saving, put this amount away in a safe place and watch it grow weekly.

Remember—food purchased in a grocery store is not taxed.

# Sample Menu of Lunches

To get you started on your money-saving journey and to make your life as simple as possible, I have created a sample month of lunches for you to try on your own; this list includes recipes from the Almost Grab and Go, Traditionalist, Creative Lunch, and Midday Gourmet sections of the book. Social Networker recipes were not included in the monthly lunch sample because these recipes also require other people to make some of the meal.

The selected recipes are economical at a cost of less than $2.50 per serving, except for the Grab and Go lunches, which will vary in price. Remember, it may cost you more to buy the list of ingredients, as it is very difficult to buy ingredients for only one or two servings of a recipe. In these cases, I advise preparing additional meals with the extra ingredients before the ingredients spoil. An option is to prepare five servings of a given recipe and then share four of the servings with four lunch friends so that you all eat the same lunch on a particular day. If your four friends agree to do the same, you can have a rotating, social lunch share for the workweek, with each person responsible for preparing a single day's lunch for the group. Then, pool your savings from not eating out in restaurants. See the Social Networker section for suggestions.

---

Since the cost and quantity vary when eating only items from the Grab and Go list, I used a $5 cost for lunch and $5 for savings. The cost price was averaged and the savings is probably lower than average because the average lunch in a restaurant including tax and tip is from $10-$15.

## Pricing

The cost pricing was determined by calculating what was spent in grocery stores and then comparing that to Shop N Cook Professional Software Version 4. Savings from a restaurant were determined by actual experience or knowing that restaurant prices are usually three times the cost of food. These prices are approximate and do vary with season, location, and type of restaurant or food store.

Remember, when using this book as a savings plan, try not to have much waste with the ingredients you purchase. Be creative and experiment with leftovers.

# 20 Days of Lunches

| Preparation | Mon | Tues | Wed | Thu | Fri | Weekly Total |
|---|---|---|---|---|---|---|
| **Cooking a whole chicken** *Page 71* | 1 Peanut Butter and Banana Wrap *Page 24* | 2 Grandma's Chicken Soup *Page 79* | 3 Chicken Caesar Wrap *Page 48* | 4 Peanut Butter, Apple, and Granola Wrap *Page 25* | 5 Tuna Parmesan Sandwich *Page 39* | |
| | Cost 1.00 **Save 3.50** | Cost 2.00 **Save 4.00** | Cost 1.50 **Save 5.50** | Cost 1.00 **Save 3.50** | Cost 2.00 **Save 4.00** | Cost $7.50 **Savings $20.50** |
| **Prepare a dozen hard-boiled eggs** *Page 94* | 6 Black Bean and Corn Salad *Page 58* | 7 5-Minute Egg Salad Sandwich *Page 33* | 8 3-5 Grab and Go items from list *Page 112* | 9 Eggplant Parmesan Sandwich (Make night before) *Page 90* | 10 Egg Salad with Apples and Almonds *Page 35* | |
| | Cost 1.00 **Save 5.00** | Cost 1.00 **Save 4.00** | Cost 5.00 **Save 5.00** | Cost 2.00 **Save 3.50** | Cost 1.50 **Save 4.00** | Cost $10.50 **Savings $21.50** |
| **Prepare Tomato and Basil Soup** *Page 81* | 11 Hummus Salad Wrap *Page 21* | 12 Tomato and Basil Soup *Page 81* | 13 Curried Egg Salad Sandwich *Page 34* | 14 Basil, Tomato, and Mozzarella Cheese Salad *Page 50* | 15 Provolone – Pesto Wrap *Page 49* | |
| | Cost 1.00 **Save 4.00** | Cost 1.50 **Save 4.00** | Cost 1.00 **Save 4.00** | Cost 1.50 **Save 4.00** | Cost 2.50 **Save 4.50** | Cost $8.00 **Savings $20.50** |
| **Prepare Vegetarian Minestrone Soup** *Page 84* | 16 Vegetarian Minestrone Soup *Page 84* | 17 Veggie and Cream Cheese Roll-Ups *Page 93* | 18 Cucumbers and Cream Cheese Sandwich *Page 29* | 19 Tuna Apple Sandwich *Page 40* | 20 Smoked Salmon and Greens *Page 51* | |
| | Cost 1.50 **Save 4.50** | Cost 1.50 **Save 3.00** | Cost 1.00 **Save 3.00** | Cost 2.50 **Save 4.00** | Cost 2.50 **Save 5.50** | Cost $9.00 **Savings $20.00** |

**Total cost for 20 days:** $ 35.00          **Total savings for 20 days:** $82.50

# All about the Recipes[1]

**Category:** Each recipe is identified by one of the five lunch styles.

**Prep and Cook Time:** Prep time is not more than 20 minutes for any recipe. The Midday Gourmet recipes may have a longer cook time.

**Serving Size:** Most recipes serve two people and if you prefer large portions, it may be a single serving for you. You can stretch it to two lunches by adding Grab and Go items.

**Food Cost (per serving):** Approximate food cost was calculated by using a combination of actual grocery receipts, and Shop N Cook Professional Software Version 4. Expect variations due to food store, season, geographic region, quantity, and inflation. The prices are also based on using all ingredients. If you make just one serving and waste the leftover food, you will be paying more than is stated for the cost of the recipe. I strongly recommend using all of the ingredients to reap the largest savings.

**Restaurant Price: Savings for one month and one year:** This section of the recipe shows how much you can save from ordering the same or similar item in a restaurant, including tip, by making it just once a week. Tax was not calculated because it varies from state to state. Savings for one month and one year are also listed.

**Ingredients:** These ingredients can be found in all grocery stores. Using organic and all-natural ingredients may cost more, but always keep a watch for sales. You can adjust the proportions of the ingredient to your taste, and if you don't have an ingredient, the recipe may still work just fine. Optional ingredients are listed in some of the recipes, but these are not calculated in the cost or savings. Feel free to experiment with new ingredients and create original lunches.

**Directions:** Each step in the directions is numbered and simply stated. You will never need to use a cooking glossary to understand the directions. Over 90% of the recipes have seven or fewer steps and none have more than ten.

---

[1] Nutritional/Personal Statement: The nutritional statement for each recipe was written by contributing author, Dr. Sara DeHart.

**Nutritional Information per serving (daily value):** The nutritional analysis was determined by using the Shop N Cook Professional Software Version 4. There may be some variations so just use the information as a guide. The daily value was based on a 2000-calorie diet. As stated in the software, "The nutritional analysis provided is not intended for medical therapy. If you are following a strict diet for medical or dietary reasons, consult first with a physician or dietician before planning your meals based on this software."

# Grab and Go Lunch Style

The Grab and Go person wants to open the refrigerator or pantry and pack what is available in a lunch container. Some of the foods may have been prepared and cooked on the weekend or for dinner the night before and require little to no preparation before eating.

Another way to create Grab and Go lunches is to think about your future lunch when you go to a restaurant. Order a larger portion of food and before you start eating, ask for a to-go container and put half of the food in the box for tomorrow's lunch. In case you don't have leftovers or go to restaurants, this section includes a Grab and Go List. The items on the list are popular favorites for lunches, but feel free to add your own favorites and customize the list for you. A blank Grab and Go List is found on page 112 so make copies and bring the list to the food store when you are doing your weekly shopping. Also use the Grab and Go List to supplement sandwich, soup, and salad recipes from the other sections.

When calculating the price of a Grab and Go lunch, use your grocery receipts or estimate between $2 and $5, which is approximately the cost of food when people make their own lunch. The Grab and Go List, ingredients for individual recipes, and Recipe Savings at a Glance are available on www.whatareyoudoingforlunch.com

### Almost Grab and Go Lunches

The nine Almost Grab and Go lunches are sandwiches made with various spreads and easy ingredients you can keep in the refrigerator. I suggest you purchase at least one spread you enjoy and create a variety of sandwiches in less than 5 minutes. The spreads suggested in the recipes include peanut butter, cream cheese, pesto, and hummus. There may be other spreads you prefer and by changing the bread, adding cucumbers, lettuce, tomatoes, and cheese, you will be amazed how tasty your lunch will be. Be creative and economical. Remember to use similar ingredients during the same week to cut down on expenses and food waste. If you find a spread you love, include it on your Grab and Go List so you remember to buy it when purchasing your lunch ingredients. I like to add at least one Grab and Go item to my brown bag for a mid-morning snack.

# Grab and Go List

Check the foods you plan to buy, and add them to your weekly shopping list. Then list them on your monthly calendar. Depending on your time and appetite, take the number of items that is right for you. I have found that three items are my good number for lunch but don't forget snack times.

**Refrigerator/Freezer**
- ☐ Hard-boiled eggs
- ☐ Healthy frozen entrées
- ☐ Hummus, pesto, guacamole, cream cheese, or peanut butter for dipping vegetables or spreading on crackers and bread
- ☐ Leftovers
- ☐ Pickles
- ☐ Yogurt (plain is healthiest)
- ☐ Other

**Fruits**
- ☐ Apples
- ☐ Bananas
- ☐ Berries
- ☐ Grapes
- ☐ Pears
- ☐ Other

**Vegetables**
- ☐ Broccoli
- ☐ Carrots
- ☐ Cauliflower
- ☐ Celery
- ☐ Cucumbers
- ☐ Greens (Dressing)
- ☐ Peppers
- ☐ Sprouts
- ☐ Snap peas
- ☐ Tomatoes
- ☐ Zucchini
- ☐ Other

**Pantry**
- ☐ Almonds, cashews, sunflower seeds
- ☐ Chips
- ☐ Crackers
- ☐ Dark chocolate bars
- ☐ Fruit leather, raisins, dried cranberries
- ☐ Healthy muffins
- ☐ Peanut butter
- ☐ Non-sweetened fruit packages
- ☐ Trail mix granola
- ☐ Other

**Drinks**
- ☐ Juices
- ☐ Water
- ☐ Other

**Spreads**
- ☐ Cream cheese
- ☐ Hummus
- ☐ Pesto
- ☐ Other

# Almost Grab and Go Recipes

# Hummus Salad Wrap

| Category: Almost Grab and Go | | Prep and Cook Time: 5 minutes | Serves: 2 |
| --- | --- | --- | --- |
| **Food Cost (per serving)** | **Restaurant Price** | **1 Month Savings** | **1 Year Savings** |
| $1.00 | $5.00 | $16.00 | $192.00 |

This is a very nutritious combination with hummus on a whole-wheat tortilla wrap layered with cheese, tomato, and lettuce. It meets 24% of your protein needs for the day. Folks of all ages loved this recipe even if they'd never tried hummus before. I recommend putting the wrap in the refrigerator before eating it at lunchtime.

**1/4 cup hummus**
**1 tomato, thinly sliced**
**2 leaves lettuce, cut up**
**2 thin slices Swiss cheese**
**2 whole-wheat or flour large tortillas (can also use bread)**

## Directions:

1. Spread hummus on entire tortilla wrap.
2. Add tomato, cheese, and lettuce to tortilla wrap.
3. Tightly roll tortilla and attach toothpick (*optional*).

**Nutritional information per serving (daily value):** Calories 263; Protein 13g (26%); Total Fat 13g (20%) (Sat. 6g (29%)); Chol. 25mg (8%); Carb. 24g (8%); Fiber 4g (15%); Sugars 3g; Calcium 279mg (28%); Iron 2mg (12%); Sodium 371mg (15%); Vit. C 12mg (20%); Vit. A 2523 IU (50%); Trans fat 0g

# Fresh Basil and Tomato Sandwich

| Category: Almost Grab and Go | Prep and Cook Time: 5 minutes | Serves: 2 |
|---|---|---|

| Food Cost (per serving) | Restaurant Price | 1 Month Savings | 1 Year Savings |
|---|---|---|---|
| $1.00 | $5.00 | $16.00 | $192.00 |

This is a delicious sandwich with only three ingredients. Basil, an aromatic herb, combines nicely with tomato to provide a vitamin-packed lunch. Purchase a potted basil plant at a farmer's market or grocery store, enjoy the fragrance in your kitchen window, and add it to lots of different foods.

**4 slices whole-wheat bread**
**8 tsp. low-fat mayonnaise**
**4 thick tomato slices**
**4 tsp. or 8 leaves of fresh basil** (found in produce section)
**salt and pepper, to taste**

## Directions:

1. Spread each slice of bread with 1 tsp. mayonnaise.
2. Top with tomato slices, 1 tsp. of fresh basil (or 4 leaves).
3. Season with salt and pepper.

**Nutritional information per serving (daily value):** Calories 273; Protein 4g (9%); Total Fat 16g (25%) (Sat. 2g (10%)); Chol. 11mg (4%); Carb. 27g (9%); Fiber 1.7g (7%); Sugars 3g; Calcium 86mg (9%); Iron 2mg (12%); Sodium 447mg (19%); Vit. C 5mg (9%); Vit. A 478 IU (10%); Trans fat 0g

# Pesto and Tomato Sandwich

| Category: Almost Grab and Go | Prep and Cook Time: 10 minutes | Serves: 2 |
|---|---|---|

| Food Cost (per serving) | Restaurant Price | 1 Month Savings | 1 Year Savings |
|---|---|---|---|
| $1.50 | $5.00 | $14.00 | $168.00 |

Pesto has a high fat-to-protein ratio but combined with fresh tomatoes, it becomes a nutritional winner. Tomatoes are value-packed with nutrition and healthful to eat every day. The cost is calculated from premade pesto, but if you are a pesto fan, try making it yourself by using the recipe provided in the Midday Gourmet section on page 78.

**4 slices whole-wheat bread**
**4-6 tbsp. prepared pesto**
**3 tbsp. plain or vanilla yogurt**
**1 thinly sliced tomato**
**salt and pepper, to taste**

## Directions:

1. Add yogurt to prepared pesto. If a toaster oven is available, place bread in oven for up to 1 to 2 minutes.
2. Spread bread with pesto and add thinly sliced tomatoes.
3. Season with salt and pepper.
4. Place sandwich in toaster oven for 2-3 more minutes (*optional*).

**Nutritional information per serving (daily value):** Calories 326; Protein 5g (10%); Total Fat 22g (30%) (Sat. 2g (30%)); Chol. 1mg (0%); Carb. 28g (9 %); Fiber 1g (4%); Sugars 6g; Calcium 115mg (11%); Iron 1mg (6%); Sodium 431mg (25%); Vit. C 12mg (20%); Vit. A 768 IU (15%); Trans fat 0g

# Peanut Butter and Banana Wrap

| Category: | Almost Grab and Go | Prep and Cook Time: | 10 minutes | Serves: | 2 |
|---|---|---|---|---|---|

| Food Cost (per serving) | Restaurant Price | 1 Month Savings | 1 Year Savings |
|---|---|---|---|
| $1.00 | $4.50 | $14.00 | $168.00 |

Peanut butter is an excellent source of protein, healthy fats, vitamins, and minerals. When combined with banana, it becomes a major source of potassium and vitamin B6. When visiting Graceland, I learned that this was one of Elvis Presley's favorite foods.

**2 sliced bananas**
**2 8-inch flour or whole-wheat tortillas**
**1/3 cup peanut butter**

## Directions:

1. Spread peanut butter on entire tortilla wrap.
2. Add sliced bananas to tortilla wrap.
3. Tightly roll tortilla and attach toothpick (*optional*).

**Nutritional information per serving (daily value):** Calories 343; Protein 12g (24%); Total Fat 22g (34%) (Sat. 5g (23%)); Chol. Omg (0%); Carb. 31g (10%); Fiber 5g (21%); Sugars 16g; Calcium 24mg (2%) Iron 1mg (6%); Sodium 198mg (8%); Vit. C 9mg (15%); Vit. A 65 IU (1%); Trans fat Og

# Peanut Butter, Apple, and Granola Wrap

| Category. Almost Grab and Go | Prep and Cook Time: 10 minutes | Serves: 2 |
| --- | --- | --- |

| Food Cost (per serving) | Restaurant Price | 1 Month Savings | 1 Year Savings |
| --- | --- | --- | --- |
| $1.00 | $4.50 | $14.00 | $168.00 |

Peanut butter combines well with apple and granola. This combination is high in protein, vitamins, minerals, fiber, and healthy fats. PB is a favorite food for people of all ages.

**2 8-inch flour tortillas**
**1/3 cup peanut butter**
**1 large apple cut in small pieces**
**1/4 cup granola**

## Directions:

1. Spread peanut butter on tortillas.
2. Add apples and sprinkle granola.
3. Tightly roll tortilla and attach toothpick (*optional*).

**Nutritional information per serving (daily value):** Calories 473; Protein 16g (32%); Total Fat 29g (43%) (Sat. 6g (29%)); Chol. 0mg (0%); Carb. 45g (15%); Fiber 6g (25%); Sugars 18g; Calcium 74mg (7%); Iron 3mg (14%); Sodium 392mg (16%); Vit. C 5mg (9%); Vit. A 44 IU (1%); Trans fat 0g

# Peanut Butter and Jelly Sandwich

| Category: Almost Grab and Go | Prep and Cook Time: 5 minutes | Serves: 2 |
|---|---|---|

| Food Cost (per serving) | Restaurant Price | 1 Month Savings | 1 Year Savings |
|---|---|---|---|
| $0.50 | $3.00 | $10.00 | $120.00 |

Peanut butter and jelly sandwiches are a comfort food that you may want to use sparingly. This is not an everyday option if you want to provide a healthy diet for yourself, your children, or your partner. Add some healthy Grab and Go items to balance out the lunch.

**4 slices whole-wheat bread**
**4 tbsp. jelly**
**4 tbsp. peanut butter**

## Directions:

1. Spread peanut butter on 1 slice of bread.
2. Spread jelly on the other slice of bread.
3. Put them together to make a sandwich.

**Nutritional information per serving (daily value):** Calories 451; Protein 12g (24%); Total Fat 18g (28%) (Sat. 4g (19%)); Chol. 0mg (0%); Carb. 66g (22%); Fiber 3g (13%); Sugars 39g; Calcium 91mg (9%); Iron 3mg (15%); Sodium 490mg (20%); Vit. C < 1mg (0%); Vit. A 0 IU (0%); Trans fat 0g

# Strawberries and Cream Cheese Sandwich

| Category: Almost Grab and Go | Prep and Cook Time: 5 minutes | Serves: 2 |
|---|---|---|

| Food Cost (per serving) | Restaurant Price | 1 Month Savings | 1 Year Savings |
|---|---|---|---|
| $1.00 | $4.50 | $14.00 | $168.00 |

Strawberries are great sources of Vitamin C and fiber. Combined with cream cheese, they add some saturated fat to your lunch but still a healthy choice for some days. Try this sandwich when fresh strawberries are available in your food market and appreciate the true taste of a strawberry. Choose organic strawberries.

**4 tbsp. cream cheese**
**4 medium strawberries, thinly sliced**
**4 slices of bread**

## Directions:

1. Spread cream cheese on two slices of bread.
2. Slice strawberries on two slices of bread.
3. Put bread with only cream cheese on top of slice with strawberries to make sandwich.

**Nutritional information per serving (daily value):** Calories 292; Protein 9g (19%); Total Fat 11g (17%) (Sat. 6g (30%)); Chol. 32mg (11%); Carb. 39g (13%); Fiber 2g (8%); Sugars 4g; Calcium 60mg (6%); Iron 3mg (14%); Sodium 509mg (21%); Vit. C 14mg (24%); Vit. A 392 IU (8%); Trans fat 0g

# Cream Cheese and Jelly Sandwich

| Category: Almost Grab and Go | Prep and Cook Time: 5 minutes | Serves: 2 |
|---|---|---|

| Food Cost (per serving) | Restaurant Price | 1 Month Savings | 1 Year Savings |
|---|---|---|---|
| $0.50 | $3.00 | $10.00 | $120.00 |

This lunch takes me back to my childhood and feeling so good seeing cream cheese and jelly wrapped up in my lunchbox. Cream cheese is satisfying and the addition of jelly makes it a sweet treat.

**4 slices bread**
**3–4 tbsp. cream cheese**
**4 tbsp. jelly**

## Directions:

1. Put cream cheese on two slices of bread.
2. Put jelly on two slices of bread.
3. Put cream cheese and jelly sides together to make a sandwich.

**Nutritional information per serving (daily value):** Calories 389; Protein 9g (19%); Total Fat 11g (17%) (Sat. 6g (30%)); Chol. 32mg (11%); Carb. 64g (21%); Fiber 2g (6%); Sugars 29g; Calcium 79mg (8%); Iron 3mg (15%); Sodium 516 mg (22%); Vit. C .13 (0%); Vit. A 389 IU (8%); Trans fat 0g

# Cucumbers and Cream Cheese Sandwich

| Category: Almost Grab and Go | | Prep and Cook Time: 5 minutes | Serves: 2 |
|---|---|---|---|
| **Food Cost (per serving)** | **Restaurant Price** | **1 Month Savings** | **1 Year Savings** |
| $1.00 | $4.00 | $12.00 | $144.00 |

Cucumbers are a very good source of vitamin C and minerals. They are also a good source of vitamin A, potassium, manganese, folate, dietary fiber, and magnesium. Cucumbers contain the important mineral silica, which is needed for bone and skin health. If cucumbers are waxed, they must be peeled but if organic and unwaxed, the skin is nutrient-rich and tasty. If you are a cream cheese fan, this is a healthier alternative to cream cheese and jelly.

**4 slices of bread**
**1/2 large cucumber**
**3-4 tbsp. cream cheese**

## Directions:

1. Spread cream cheese on each slice of bread.
2. Cut cucumber in thin slices.
3. Add cucumber to top of cream cheese to create sandwich.

**Nutritional information per serving (daily value):** Calories 288; Protein 9g (19%); Total Fat 11g (17%) (Sat. 6g (30%)); Chol. 32mg (11%); Carb. 38g (13%); Fiber 2g (8%); Sugars 3g; Calcium 61mg (6%); Iron 3mg (14%); Sodium 510mg (21%); Vit. C 91mg (2%); Vit. A 419 IU (8%); Trans fat 0%

# *Traditionalist* Lunch Style

The Traditionalist is willing to spend 15-20 minutes in the morning or the night before making lunch for the upcoming workday. These recipes are the "old standbys" that are familiar and comfortable to make. In this section, you will find ingredients with interesting yet easy ways to use them. Included are sandwiches and wraps for egg salad, tuna salad, and meat and cheese variations. Changing the type of bread you are using and adding a variety of cheeses and vegetables can really help vary your lunches.

# Traditionalist Recipes

# 5-Minute Egg Salad Sandwich

| Category: Traditionalist | Prep and Cook Time: 10 minutes | | Serves: 2 |
|---|---|---|---|
| **Food Cost (per serving)** | **Restaurant Price** | **1 Month Savings** | **1 Year Savings** |
| $1.00 | $5.00 | $16.00 | $192.00 |

Hard-boiled eggs are a good source of Vitamin A and protein. Unfortunately, eggs are also a rich source of cholesterol so don't select eggs for both breakfast and lunch. If you are an egg salad fan and want to know what is put into egg salads, you will like this easy and quick recipe.

**3 eggs**
**4 slices of bread or rolls**
**2 tbsp. mayonnaise**
**1/2 tsp. Dijon mustard**

## Directions:

1. In medium bowl stir together the mayonnaise and Dijon mustard.
2. Chop the eggs with a fork and mix with mayonnaise/mustard.
3. Create sandwich.

*Optional*: Add 2 tbsp. of onion, and/or 2 tbsp. of relish, lettuce, and/or tomatoes. Serve as salad on a bed of greens.

**Nutritional information per serving (daily value):** Calories 391; Protein 17g (34%); Total Fat 20g (30%) (Sat. 4g (19%)); Chol. 325mg (108%); Carb. 37g (12%); Fiber 2g (6%); Sugars 2g; Calcium 70mg (7%); Iron 4g (15%); Sodium 599mg (25%); Vit. C < 1mg (0%); Vit. A 404 IU (8%); Trans fat 0g

# Curried Egg Salad Sandwich

| Category: Traditionalist | | Prep and Cook Time: 15 minutes | | Serves: 2 |
|---|---|---|---|---|
| **Food Cost (per serving)** | **Restaurant Price** | | **1 Month Savings** | **1 Year Savings** |
| $1.00 | $5.00 | | $16.00 | $192.00 |

If you love egg salad and are tired of the same old sandwich, try this variation with just a little curry powder. It's a tasty, high-protein sandwich, but be aware that the fat content is somewhat high.

> **4 hard-boiled eggs**
> **4 slices of bread**
> **2 tbsp mayonnaise (add more if necessary)**
> **1 tsp. curry powder**
> **salt and pepper, to taste**

## Directions:

1. Mix together the curry powder and the mayonnaise in a medium bowl.
2. Chop the eggs until pieces are small, then add to the curry powder and mayonnaise. Add salt and pepper, to taste.
3. Create sandwich.

*Optional*: Add lettuce and/or tomatoes. Serve as salad on a bed of greens.

**Nutritional information per serving (daily value):** Calories 241; Protein 13g (25%); Total Fat 21g (32%) (Sat. 4g (2 1%)); Chol. 431mg (144%); Carb. 1g (0%); Fiber 2g (6%); Sugars 1g; Calcium 58mg (6%); Iron 2g (11%); Sodium 634mg (30%); Vit. C < 1mg (0%); Vit. A 526 IU (11%); Trans fat 0g

# Egg Salad with Apples and Almonds

| Category: Traditionalist | Prep and Cook Time: 15 minutes | Serves: 2 |
|---|---|---|

| Food Cost (per serving) | Restaurant Price | 1 Month Savings | 1 Year Savings |
|---|---|---|---|
| $1.50 | $5.50 | $16.00 | $192.00 |

Egg salad with yogurt rather than mayo is a taste delight. Eggs are protein- and cholesterol-dense, which means that this lunch should be varied with other selections in this book. The addition of apple and almonds make this dish especially nutritious.

**4 hard-boiled eggs**
**1/2 tsp. curry powder**
**3 tbsp. plain yogurt**
**1 small onion cut in small pieces**

**1 small apple, cut into small pieces**
**1/4 cup almonds, toasted and chopped**
**salt and pepper, to taste**
**2 large lettuce leaves (Use more for larger lunch)**

## Directions:

1. Mix yogurt, curry powder, and salt in small bowl.
2. Crack and peel each egg and place in a medium bowl and chop eggs with a fork, then add the curry powder, yogurt, onions, apple, and almonds. Mix together; if it needs more moisture, add more yogurt a little at a time.
3. Spread on lettuce leaves.
4. Add salt and pepper, to taste.

**Nutritional information per serving (daily value):** Calories 225; Protein 16g (33%); Total Fat 11g (17%) (Sat. 4g (18%)); Chol. 425mg (142%); Carb. 18g (6%); Fiber 3g (14%); Sugars 11g; Calcium 145mg (15%); Iron 3g (14%); Sodium 191mg (8%); Vit. C 31mg (3%); Vit. A 10907 IU (218%); Trans fat 0g

# Ham and Cheese Wrap

| Category: Traditionalist | Prep and Cook Time: 10 minutes | Serves: 2 |
|---|---|---|

| Food Cost (per serving) | Restaurant Price | 1 Month Savings | 1 Year Savings |
|---|---|---|---|
| $3.00 | $7.00 | $16.00 | $192.00 |

Ham and cheese wraps are filling and satisfying when a hearty lunch is desired. It's easy to create new wraps by just changing the type of meat and cheese.

**2 large tortillas (whole-wheat or flour)**
**4 tbsp cream cheese**
**1/2 tsp. garlic powder**
**4 oz. sliced cooked ham**
**1/2 cup lettuce**
**1 medium tomato, thinly sliced**
**2 oz. Colby Jack cheese**

## Directions:

1. Spread each tortilla with a thin layer of cream cheese.
2. Sprinkle lightly with garlic powder.
3. Layer one side of each tortilla with two slices of cheese and slices of ham.
4. Top with lettuce and tomatoes.
5. Roll up each tortilla. Use toothpicks if necessary.

**Nutritional information per serving (daily value):** Calories 406; Protein 24g (48%); Total Fat 26g (39%) (Sat. 13g (67%)); Chol. 92mg (31%); Carb. 20g (7%); Fiber 2g (7%); Sugars 3g; Calcium 280mg (28%); Iron 2mg (13%); Sodium 1234mg (51%); Vit. C 8mg (14%); Vit. A1502 IU (30%); Trans fat 0g

# Pita Bread Meat and Cheese Sandwich

| Category: Traditionalist | Prep and Cook Time: 15 minutes | Serves: 2 |
|---|---|---|

| Food Cost (per serving) | Restaurant Price | 1 Month Savings | 1 Year Savings |
|---|---|---|---|
| $3.00 | $7.00 | $16.00 | $192.00 |

A meat and cheese sandwich is a hearty lunch selection that should be varied with fresh fruits and vegetables.

**1/4 cup Dijon mustard and mayonnaise blend**
**(mix proportions according to your taste)**
**1 tbsp. honey**
**2 pita sandwich bread**
**2 oz. sliced cheddar cheese**
**4 oz. sliced turkey or ham**
**1 apple, thinly sliced**

## Directions:

1. Combine mustard and mayonnaise and mix with honey.
2. Spread on the inside of pita bread.
3. Put cheese, meat, and apple in pita bread.

**Nutritional information per serving (daily value):** Calories 430; Protein 28g (56%); Total Fat 27g (41%) (Sat. 14g (70%)); Chol. 88 mg (29%); Carb. 19g (6%); Fiber 2g (8%); Sugars 1g; Calcium 465 mg (46%); Iron 2mg (13%) Sodium 1609mg (67%); Vit. C .5mg (1%); Vit. A 583 IU (12%); Trans fat .004g

# Famous Tuna Salad Sandwich

| Category: | Traditionalist | Prep and Cook Time: | 20 minutes | Serves: | 2 |
|---|---|---|---|---|---|

| Food Cost (per serving) | Restaurant Price | 1 Month Savings | 1 Year Savings |
|---|---|---|---|
| $2.00 | $6.00 | $16.00 | $192.00 |

The nutritional value and taste of tuna salad is dependent on the ingredients. Tuna canned in water is preferable to oil-based selections, and low-fat mayo is preferable to regular mayonnaise. When making the sandwich at home, you are sure of the ingredients.

**1 can water-packed tuna (6-1/2 or 7 oz.)**
**1 hard-boiled egg, mashed**
**1 tbsp. onion cut in small**
**1 tbsp. celery cut in small pieces**

**1 tomato, sliced**
**1 tsp. Dijon mustard**
**1 tbsp. mayonnaise**
**1/2 tsp. salt**
**2 lettuce leaves in small pieces**
**4 slices of bread**

## Directions:

1. In a medium bowl, place tuna, egg, onion, celery, mustard, mayonnaise, and salt.
2. With a fork, combine all ingredients well.
3. Put the lettuce leaves on 2 slices of bread and put the sandwich mix on the other 2 slices of bread.

**Nutritional information per serving (daily value):** Calories 454; Protein 37g (73%); Total Fat 16g (25%) (Sat. 3g (15%)); Chol. 125mg (42%); Carb. 40g (13%); Fiber 3g (10%); Sugars 4g; Calcium 69mg (7%); Iron 4g (15%); Sodium 803mg (33%); Vit. C 12mg (20%); Vit.A 2496 IU (50%); Trans fat 0g

# Tuna Parmesan Sandwich

| Category: Traditionalist | Prep and Cook Time: 10 minutes | Serves: 2 |
|---|---|---|

| Food Cost (per serving) | Restaurant Price | 1 Month Savings | 1 Year Savings |
|---|---|---|---|
| $2.00 | $6.00 | $16.00 | $192.00 |

Homemade tuna salad is about 50% fat and 38% protein, so it is a lunch that should be varied with other foods. Don't eat tuna salad sandwiches every day, but it is a good nutritious choice for some lunches.

**1 can water-packed tuna (6-1/2 or 7 oz.)**
**4 slices of bread**
**4 tbsp. mayonnalse or salad dressing**
**1 tbsp. grated Parmesan cheese**
**1/2 tsp. curry powder**

## Directions:

1. In a medium bowl, stir together the tuna, mayonnaise, Parmesan cheese, and season with curry powder. Mix well.
2. Spread 1 tbsp, mayonnaise on bread, and put tuna mixture on top of each slice.

*Optional*: Spread on a bed of greens instead of using bread for a delicious salad.

**Nutritional information per serving (daily value):** Calories 593; Protein 38g (76%); Total Fat 32g (50%) (Sat. 5g (24%)); Chol. 37mg (12%); Carb. 37g (12%); Fiber 2g (6%); Sugars 2g; Calcium 96mg (19%); Iron 4g (15%); Sodium 986mg (41%); Vlt. C < Img (0%); Vit. A 186 IU (4%); Trans fat 0g

# Tuna Apple Sandwich

| Category: Traditionalist | Prep and Cook Time: 15 minutes | | Serves: 2 |
|---|---|---|---|
| **Food Cost (per serving)** | **Restaurant Price** | **1 Month Savings** | **1 Year Savings** |
| $2.50 | $6.50 | $16.00 | $192.00 |

Tuna is an excellent source of protein and omega-3 fatty acids, but there are concerns about mercury lodged in that big fish's muscle cells. This is not an every day-for-lunch option, but with apple and celery it is tasty and filled with good nutrients. This is one lunch that is much better prepared at home rather than prepared at a restaurant or take-out service because you can adjust the amount of mayo, thereby controlling the total fat content.

**2 tbsp, mayonnaise**
**1/4 cup finely chopped celery**
**1/4 cup finely chopped walnuts**
**2 tbsp. finely chopped onion**
**1 can water-packed tuna (6-1/2 or 7 oz.)**
**1 red apple cut in small pieces**
**4 slices bread**
**4 lettuce leaves**

## Directions:

1. In a large bowl, combine the first four ingredients; stir in tuna and apple.
2. Spread tuna mixture on pieces of bread.
3. Top with lettuce and remaining bread.

**Nutritional information per serving (daily value):** Calories 572; Protein 31g (62%); Total Fat 26g (40%) (Sat. 4g (18%)); Chol. 40mg (13%); Carb. 57g (19%); Fiber 5g (20%); Sugars 15g; Calcium 83mg (8%); Iron 4g (15%); Sodium 553mg (23%); Vit. C 0.15mg (25%); Vit. A 5543 IU (111%); Trans fat 0g

# Creative Lunch Style

The Creative lunch style is for a person willing to try new recipes and either spends 15-20 minutes in the morning or the night before making lunch for the upcoming day. Included in this category are sandwiches and wraps, salads, smoothies, and snacks. This type of person is willing to try new recipes.

Always refer back to lunch suggestions in the Almost Grab and Go and Traditionalist sections before deciding on your lunch menu. Think about how hungry you are at lunchtime, and remember to add one to three Grab and Go items with your selection. When calculating your cost of lunch, don't forget to add Grab and Go items in your final cost.

# Creative Lunch Recipes

# Shrimp Salad Sandwich

| Category: Creative | Prep and Cook Time: 15 minutes | Serves: 2 |
|---|---|---|

| Food Cost (per serving) | Restaurant Price | 1 Month Savings | 1 Year Savings |
|---|---|---|---|
| $4.00 | $7.50 | $14.00 | $168.00 |

It was a popular myth in the 1990s that shrimp raised cholesterol levels. Not true, say nutrition experts. Shrimp is low in fat and calories and also offers beneficial doses of omega-3 fatty acids, vitamin B12, and niacin. Shrimp also are mineral-rich, supplying iron, zinc, and copper. This special sandwich goes well with a variety of fresh fruits.

**3 tbsp. soft cream cheese**
**1 tsp. lemon juice**
**1 tbsp. chopped onion**
**1/2 lb. small cooked shrimp, peeled**

**2 Roma tomatoes, sliced**
**1 c. shredded lettuce**
**4 pieces of bread (French bread is my favorite for this sandwich)**

## Directions:

1. Mix the first three ingredients together in a medium bowl.
2. Add cooked and peeled shrimp.
3. Top bread with lettuce, tomato slices, and shrimp mixture.

*Optional*: If mixture seems dry, add a small amount of mayonnaise to the bread.

**Nutritional information per serving (daily value):** Calories 394; Protein 32g (65%); Total Fat 11g (16%) (Sat.5g (25%)); Chol. 194mg (65%); Carb. 41g (14%); Fiber 3g (10%); Sugars 4g; Calcium 122mg (12%); Iron 5mg (30%); Sodium 660mg (28%); Vit. C 15mg (24%); Vit. A 2343 IU (47%); Trans fat 0g

# Curried Chicken Salad

| Category: Creative | Prep and Cook Time: 15 minutes | Serves: 4 |
|---|---|---|

| Food Cost (per serving) | Restaurant Price | 1 Month Savings | 1 Year Savings |
|---|---|---|---|
| $3.00 | $7.50 | $18.00 | $216.00 |

Chicken is a protein-dense food and if you make your own chicken salad, you have control over the caloric value. Curry is a healthy spice that has anti-inflammatory properties. If you want an easy salad, just add the chicken salad to a bed of greens.

**2 cups cubed cooked chicken**
**1/2 cup chopped celery**
**2 tbsp. mayonnaise**
**1/4 cup sour cream**

**3 tbsp. lemon juice**
***1–2 tbsp. curry powder**
**salt and pepper, to taste**
**4 pieces of whole-wheat bread, tortilla, or roll**

* Vary proportions of curry powder according to your personal taste..

## Directions:

1. In a large bowl, combine chicken and celery.
2. In a separate bowl, combine mayonnaise, sour cream, lemon juice, curry powder, and salt and pepper, to taste.
3. Add mayonnaise mixture to the large bowl of chicken and celery. Blend well.
4. Serve on bread, tortillas, or rolls or on a bed of greens.

**Nutritional information per serving (daily value):** Calories 510; Protein 25g (51%); Total Fat 32g (49%) (Sat. 6g (29%)); Chol. 86mg (29%); Carb. 30g (10%); Fiber 3g (12%); Sugars 4g; Calcium 141mg (14%); Iron 4mg (22%); Sodium 608 (25%); Vit. C 5mg (8%); Vit. A 438 IU (9%); Trans fat 0g

# Grandma's Chicken Salad Sandwich

| Category: Creative | Prep and Cook Time: 15 minutes | Serves: 4 |
|---|---|---|

| Food Cost (per serving) | Restaurant Price | 1 Month Savings | 1 Year Savings |
|---|---|---|---|
| $3.50 | $7.50 | $16.00 | $192.00 |

Chicken salad is an excellent source of protein and fiber, but use sparingly if you need to watch fat caloric intake. This is the traditional chicken salad I loved when my grandma made it.

**2 cups cut-up cooked chicken**
**1/2 cup diced celery**
**3 tbsp. green onions**
**1/2 cup mayonnaise**
**2 tsp. lemon juice**
**salt and pepper, to taste**
**4 pieces whole-wheat bread**

## Directions:

1. Combine chicken with next 4 ingredients in a mixing bowl. Taste-test, and if it is too dry, add more mayonnaise sparingly.
2. Salt and pepper, to taste.
3. You can put the chicken salad on lettuce if you are not in the mood for a sandwich.

**Nutritional information per serving (daily value):** Calories 299; Protein 5g (10%); Total Fat 22g (35%) (Sat. 3g (13%)); Chol. 19mg (6%); Carb. 20g (7%); Fiber 1g (4%); Sugars 2g; Calcium 28mg (3%); Iron 1mg (8%); Sodium 380mg (16%); Vit. C 2mg (3%); Vit. A 327 IU (7%); Trans fat 0g

# Chicken/Turkey Caesar Wrap

| Category: Creative | Prep and Cook Time: 5 minutes | Serves: 2 |
|---|---|---|

| Food Cost (per serving) | Restaurant Price | 1 Month Savings | 1 Year Savings |
|---|---|---|---|
| $1.50 | $7.00 | $22.00 | $264.00 |

This is a good source of protein for those who do not need to watch their fat intake. This easy recipe makes you feel like you're a real chef.

**2 (8-inch) wheat or flour tortillas**
**1/2 head cut or shredded lettuce**
**1 1/2 cup cooked or canned chicken or turkey, thinly sliced**
**1/2 small red onion, thinly sliced**
**1/4 cup grated Parmesan cheese**
**6 tbsp. bottled Caesar dressing**

## Directions:

1. Layer lettuce, meat, and onion at center of tortilla.
2. Drizzle dressing and sprinkle with Parmesan cheese.
3. Wrap and secure with toothpicks.

**Nutritional information per serving (daily value):** Calories 420; Protein 30g (62%); Total Fat 42g (51%) (Sat. 6 (31%)); Chol. 116 mg (39%); Carb. 4g (1%); Fiber 1.8g (7%); Sugars 2g; Calcium 69 mg (7%); Iron 2.4 mg (14%); Sodium 295mg (12%); Vit. C 2mg (3%); Vit. A 455 IU (9%); Trans fat 0g

# Provolone-Pesto Wrap

| Category: Creative | Prep and Cook Time: 15 minutes | Serves: 2 |
|---|---|---|

| Food Cost (per serving) | Restaurant Price | 1 Month Savings | 1 Year Savings |
|---|---|---|---|
| $2.50 | $7.00 | $18.00 | $216.00 |

This wrap makes a tasty, creative, and nutritious lunch. It is a great recipe when you aren't sure if you want a sandwich or salad. One of the recipe testers used her recipe creativity. "I thought this recipe was great! I used Provolone once, but then started using Havarti cheese for a creamier taste. I also used small tomatoes and about a tablespoon of sour cream and a tablespoon of pesto for a single sandwich. I used only spinach leaves but romaine lettuce would have been good too." I encourage you to experiment and create new lunches with all the recipes.

**1/2 cup light sour cream**
**1/4 cup reduced-fat pesto**
**2 whole-wheat or flour tortillas (8-inch)**

**2 cups packed fresh spinach leaves – washed, stems removed**
**1 large tomato, thinly sliced**
**1/4 lb. Provolone cheese**

## Directions:

1. In a small bowl, mix sour cream and pesto.
2. Spread evenly over tortilla.
3. Layer tortillas with spinach, tomato slices, and cheese.
4. Roll up tortillas and secure with toothpicks.

**Nutritional information per serving (daily value):** Calories 418; Protein 19g (39%); Total Fat 29g (44%) (Sat. 17g (84%)); Chol .69mg (23%); Carb. 22g (7%); Fiber 2g (9%); Sugars 5g; Calcium 561 mg (56%); Iron 2mg (13%); Sodium 754mg (31%); Vit. C 16mg (27%); Vit. A 4130 IU (83%); Trans fat 0g

# Basil, Tomato, and Mozzarella Cheese Salad

| Category: Creative | Prep and Cook Time: 10 minutes | Serves: 2 |
|---|---|---|

| Food Cost (per serving) | Restaurant Price | 1 Month Savings | 1 Year Savings |
|---|---|---|---|
| $1.50 | $5.50 | $16.00 | $192.00 |

Aromatic herb goodness combined with tomato sets off this Mozzarella cheese salad. When basil is in season, buy a fresh potted plant and add the leaves to other salads and sandwiches.

**2 medium tomatoes**
**1/2 head of lettuce**
**8 leaves fresh basil**
**2 oz. thinly sliced Mozzarella cheese**
**2 tsp. olive oil**
**salt and pepper, to taste**

## Directions:

1. Slice tomatoes into 1/2-inch-thick slices.
2. Place cut-up lettuce on bottom of lunch container.
3. Place tomatoes on top of lettuce.
4. Place fresh basil leaves on top of the tomatoes.
5. Place sliced Mozzarella cheese over basil.
6. Pour olive oil over the top of the salad and add salt and pepper, to taste. You may want to pour the olive oil over the salad just before eating.

**Nutritional information per serving (daily value):** Calories 159; Protein 9g (17%); Total Fat 11g (17%) (Sat. 4g (22%)); Chol. 22mg (7%); Carb. 8g (3%); Fiber 3g (11%); Sugars 4g; Calcium 190mg (19%); Iron 1.3mg (7%); Sodium 207mg (9%); Vit. C 32g (54%); Vit. A 7983 IU (160%); Trans fat 0g

# Smoked Salmon and Greens

| Category: Creative | Prep and Cook Time: 15 minutes | Serves: 2 |
|---|---|---|

| Food Cost (per serving) | Restaurant Price | 1 Month Savings | 1 Year Savings |
|---|---|---|---|
| $2.50 | $8.00 | $22.00 | $264.00 |

Use wild salmon rather than farm-harvested for the best taste and nutrition. Salmon is an excellent source of protein and omega-3 fatty acids, which are great for the skin as well as smooth blood flow. Greens add vitamins and minerals that our bodies need every day. This elegant salad is a wonderful side dish with a bowl of soup, especially on a cold day.

**3 cups cut-up greens**
**1/4 lb. smoked salmon, cut in small pieces**
**1 apple, chopped in small pieces**
**1/4 lb. Jack cheese, diced**
**6 tbsp. commercial organic raspberry vinaigrette dressing**
  **(vary amount to taste)**
*Optional*: **croutons**

## Directions:

1. Place three cups of washed greens in bowl
2. Add the next three ingredients.
3. Add salad dressing when serving.

*If you are packing your lunch, put dressing in small container and pour over salad just before eating.

**Nutritional information per serving (daily value) *without salad dressing:** Calories 324; Protein 25g (50%; Total Fat 19g (30%) (Sat. 11g(56%)); Chol. 62 (21%); Carb. 13g (4%); Fiber 2g (8%); Sugars 9g; Calcium 453mg (45%); Iron 2 mg (9%); Sodium 759mg (32%); Vit. C 16mg (27%); Vit. A 5841 IU (117%); Trans fat 0

# Tuna Avocado Salad

| Category: Creative | Prep and Cook Time: 15 minutes | Serves: 2 |
|---|---|---|

| Food Cost (per serving) | Restaurant Price | 1 Month Savings | 1 Year Savings |
|---|---|---|---|
| $2.00 | $7.50 | $22.00 | $264.00 |

Tuna and avocado are a winning combination. Avocados provide nearly 20 essential nutrients, including fiber, potassium, Vitamin E, B vitamins, and folic acid. They also act as a "nutrient booster" by enabling the body to absorb more fat-soluble nutrients. When sliced fresh fruit is added to the salad, it becomes a nutritious powerhouse.

**1 can tuna (6-1/2 or 7 oz.)**
**1 egg, hard-boiled and chopped**
**2 tsp. regular mustard**
**1 tbsp. mayonnaise**
**1 tsp. onion, finely chopped**
**1 tbsp. celery, finely chopped**

**1/2 tsp. sea salt**
**1/2 tsp. pepper**
**1 tomato, sliced**
**1 avocado, halved**
**2 lettuce leaves**

## Directions:

1. In a medium bowl, place first eight ingredients and combine with a fork.
2. Cut avocado in half; remove the pit and scoop out pieces of avocado.
3. Place tuna mixture in avocado shell and put scooped-out avocado on cut-up lettuce leaves on the side of avocado.
4. Add sliced tomatoes to avocado and lettuce.

**Nutritional information per serving (daily value):** Calories 436; Protein 31g (63%); Total Fat 30g (46%) (Sat. 5g (24%)); Chol. 125 (42%); Carb. 13g (9%); Fiber 8g (33%); Sugars 3g; Calcium 60mg (6%); Iron 3mg (16%); Sodium 1045mg (44%); Vit. C 23mg (38%); Vit. A 2665 IU (53%); Trans fat 0g

# Spinach Salad with Feta and Walnuts

| Category: Creative | Prep and Cook Time: 15 minutes | Serves: 2 |
|---|---|---|

| Food Cost (per serving) | Restaurant Price | 1 Month Savings | 1 Year Savings |
|---|---|---|---|
| $2.00 | $7.50 | $22.00 | $264.00 |

Spinach is a high-value phytonutrient vegetable that offers a wide range of benefits to most of our physiological processes. Feta cheese and walnuts round out this salad to treat the taste buds. This delicious recipe is so easy to create, and people who usually pass on salads like this one.

**3 tbsp. olive oil**
**2 tbsp. balsamic vinegar**
**1/2 cup toasted walnuts, broken into small pieces**
**5 oz. spinach, washed (remove stems and pat dry)**
**1/4 cup Feta cheese, crumbled**

## Directions:

1. Mix together the olive oil and balsamic vinegar, and refrigerate.
2. Put walnuts on a cookie sheet and place under a broiler for 3 minutes or until brown and toasted (walnuts burn easily, so time carefully).
3. While walnuts are toasting, wash spinach, remove stems, and place in bowl.
4. Add toasted walnuts to spinach.
5. Complete the salad by mixing in the Feta cheese and salad dressing.

**Nutritional information per serving (daily value):** Calories 300; Protein 6g (12%); Total Fat 29g (45%) (Sat. 5g (25%)); Chol. 11 mg (4%); Carb. 7g (2%); Fiber 2g (9%); Sugars 2g; Calcium 130mg (13%); Iron 2mg (11%); Sodium 179mg (7%); Vit. C 13mg (22%); Vit. A 4433 IU (89%); Trans fat 0g

# Strawberry/Mango Salad

| Category: Creative | Prep and Cook Time: 15 minutes | Serves: 2 |
|---|---|---|

| Food Cost (per serving) | Restaurant Price | 1 Month Savings | 1 Year Savings |
|---|---|---|---|
| $2.00 | $8.00 | $24.00 | $288.00 |

Strawberries and mangos both are high in nutritional value. Strawberries have more vitamin C than some citrus fruits. They are also high in fiber, folate, potassium, and antioxidants. Mango is a powerful antioxidant and valued for its anticancer properties. Mixed together with a couple of other ingredients, this salad makes a quick and tasty lunch.

**1/8 cup balsamic vinegar**
**1/2 cup canola oil**
**1/4 cup sugar**
**1/2 tsp. salt**
**4 cups torn greens**
**1/4 lb. strawberries, quartered**

**1/2 mango peeled (seeded and cut in small pieces)**
**1/2 cup dried cranberries**
**1/4 onion, sliced in small pieces**
**1/4 cup almond pieces**

## Directions:

1. Place vinegar, oil, sugar and salt in a jar with lid, and shake well.
2. In a bowl, mix greens, strawberries, mango, cranberries, and onion.
3. When ready to eat, add dressing and top with almonds.

**Nutritional information per serving (daily value):** Calories 411; Protein 2g (4%); Total Fat 30g (47%) (Sat. 2g (11%)); Chol. 0mg (0%); Carb. 36g (12%); Fiber 3g (13%); Sugars 30g; Calcium 41mg (4%); Iron 2mg (9%); Sodium 308mg (13%); Vit. C 31mg (51%); Vit. A 2867 IU (57%); Trans fat 0.1g.

# Classic Caesar Salad

| Category: Creative | Prep and Cook Time: 15 minutes | Serves: 4 |
|---|---|---|

| Food Cost (per serving) | Restaurant Price | 1 Month Savings | 1 Year Savings |
|---|---|---|---|
| $2.50 | $7.50 | $20.00 | $240.00 |

This is an elegant salad with somewhat higher caloric content than a plain salad, but the taste improvement may be worth it. The vitamin-mineral content is excellent. If you love Caesar's salads in restaurants, this recipe will be one of your favorites. There is enough Caesar's salad to share or have for a dinner.

- **1 large head of romaine lettuce, rinsed, dried, and torn Into bite-sized pieces**
- **3 large garlic cloves, peeled and crushed**
- **4 tbsp. commercial Caesar salad dressing**

- **1/2 cup grated Parmesan cheese**
- **1/2 cup croutons**
- **salt and pepper, to taste**
- ***Optional*: anchovies**

## Directions:

1. Place lettuce in a large bowl.
2. Add crushed garlic, and mix with lettuce.
3. Add Parmesan cheese and croutons.
4. Salt and pepper to taste.

Bring salad dressing in a container and pour on right before eating.

**Nutritional Information per serving (daily value):** Calories 367; Protein 6g (12%); Total Fat 33g (50%) (Sat. 6g (29%)); Chol. 11mg (4%); Carb. 14g (5%); Fiber 1g (4%); Sugars 11g; Calcium 168mg (17%); Iron 1mg (6%); Sodium 755mg (31%); Vit C 11mg (18%); Vit. A 3454 IU (69%); Trans fat 0g

# Mixed Green Salad

| Category: Creative | Prep and Cook Time: 15 minutes | Serves: 4 |
|---|---|---|

| Food Cost (per serving) | Restaurant Price | 1 Month Savings | 1 Year Savings |
|---|---|---|---|
| $1.50 | $6.00 | $18.00 | $216.00 |

Leafy vegetables are a good choice for a healthful diet because they are naturally low in calories and sodium. Many of the health benefits that leafy greens provide come from phytonutrients – unique compounds that provide protection for plants and act as antioxidants for humans. Antioxidants help prevent cancer and heart disease. If you want to lose weight, check the calorie count of your favorite dressings and go easy with the bottle.

**1 head romaine lettuce
1 cucumber, peeled and sliced
2 or 3 plum tomatoes, cored and cut into small pieces
1 small red onion, sliced thin
salt and pepper to taste
*Favorite salad dressing**

## Directions:

1. Tear lettuce into bite-size pieces and transfer them to a large salad bowl.
2. Add the cucumber, tomatoes, and onion.
3. Add favorite salad dressing, salt, and pepper, and toss before serving.

**Nutritional information per serving (daily value) *without salad dressing:** Calories 53; Protein 3g (6%); Total Fat 1g (1%) (Sat.109g (1%)); Chol. 0mg (0%); Carb. 11g (4%); Fiber 5g (18%); Sugars 5g; Calcium 72mg (7%); Iron 2mg (11%); Sodium 17mg (1%); Vit. C 47mg (78%); Vit. A 14098 IU (282%); Trans fat 0g

# Fruit and Nut Salad

| Category: Creative | Prep and Cook Time: 15 minutes | | Serves: 4 |
|---|---|---|---|
| **Food Cost (per serving)** | **Restaurant Price** | **1 Month Savings** | **1 Year Savings** |
| $2.00 | $7.50 | $22.00 | $264.00 |

Fruits are absolutely essential to a healthy diet. This is a healthy choice for some lunches. I found when I use at least three fruits that are in season served over lettuce with the dressing in this recipe, the lunch is great.

**1 small apple, thinly sliced**
**1 small pear, thinly sliced**
**1 orange, peeled and sliced**
**1/3 cup canola oil**

**3 tbsp. white wine vinegar**
**1 tbsp. honey**
**1/4 cup slivered almonds**
**2-4 lettuce leaves**

## Directions:

1. In a large bowl, combine sliced fruits.
2. In a small bowl, blend oil, vinegar, and honey.
3. Pour dressing over fruit, and toss.
4. Place lettuce on a plate or lunch container, and put fruit on top of lettuce.
5. Sprinkle with slivered almonds.

**Nutritional information per serving (daily value):** Calories 154; Protein 2g (2%); Total Fat 9g (13%) (Sat. 7g (4%)); Chol. 0mg (0%); Carb. 20g (7%); Fiber 4g (16%); Sugars 14g; Calcium 41mg (4%); Iron 7mg (4%); Sodium 5mg (0%); Vit. C 22mg (37%); Vit. A 1281 IU (26%); Trans fat .001g

# Black Bean and Corn Salad

| Category: Creative | Prep and Cook Time: 20 minutes | Serves: 5 |
|---|---|---|

| Food Cost (per serving) | Restaurant Price | 1 Month Savings | 1 Year Savings |
|---|---|---|---|
| $1.00 | $6.00 | $20.00 | $240.00 |

Beans and corn are excellent sources of protein. This dish is easy to prepare and is a great leftover. It can be used as a main lunch salad or several side salads during the week.

**1 14-oz. can black beans**
**1 cup frozen corn**
**1 small red pepper, chopped (*optional*)**
**1/2 red onion, chopped**
**2 tbsp. olive oil**
**3 large lettuce leaves**
**salt and pepper to taste**

## Directions:

1. Combine all ingredients in a medium bowl. Let stand for at least 15 minutes before eating for corn to defrost and flavors to combine.
2. Toss the salad.
3. Put on three large lettuce leaves.

**Nutritional information per serving (daily value):** Calories 149; Protein 5g (11%); Total Fat 6g (9%) (Sat. 0.09g (5%)); Chol. 0mg (0%); Carb. 20g (32%); Fiber 5g (21%); Sugars 2g; Calcium 36mg (4%); Iron 1.23mg (7%); Sodium 233mg (10%); Vit. C 6mg (11%); Vit. A 10661 IU (21%); Trans fat 0g

# Mango Smoothie

| Category: Creative | Prep and Cook Time: 10 minutes | Serves: 2 |
|---|---|---|

| Food Cost (per serving) | Restaurant Price | 1 Month Savings | 1 Year Savings |
|---|---|---|---|
| $2.00 | $5.00 | $12.00 | $144.00 |

Mango is an antioxidant and anticancer fruit. When prepared in a smoothie, it becomes a healthy, delicious, and easy meal or snack. Add Grab and Go item(s) for a larger lunch.

**2 large mangos, pitted and peeled**
**1 bunch of parsley, de-stemmed**

## Directions:

1. Put ingredients in juicer or blender.
2. Add 2 cups of water.
3. Mix on high speed.

**Nutritional information per serving (daily value):** Calories 84; Protein 2g (4%); Total Fat .52g (1%) Sat. 0.9g (0%)); Chol. 0mg (0%); Carb. 8g (3%); Fiber 2g (9%); Sugars 5g; Calcium 80mg (19%); Iron 4mg (19%); Sodium 32mg (1%); Vit. C 82mg (137%); Vit. A 4931 IU (99%); Trans fat 0g

# Fruit and Greens Smoothie

| Category: Creative | Prep and Cook Time: 10 minutes | Serves: 2 |
| --- | --- | --- |

| Food Cost (per serving) | Restaurant Price | 1 Month Savings | 1 Year Savings |
| --- | --- | --- | --- |
| $1.50 | $4.00 | $10.00 | $120.00 |

This combination is an excellent source of vitamins and minerals. Some people do not enjoy eating greens, but try drinking them for a real taste treat. Bring this great snack or lunch when you are on the go.

**1 cup apple juice**
**1 banana, peeled**
**1 mango, pitted and peeled**
**5 kale leaves or other greens (remove stems before putting in juicer or blender)**

## Directions:

1. Put ingredients in juicer or blender.
2. Add 1 cup of water.
3. Mix on high speed.

**Nutritional information per serving (daily value):** Calories 354; Protein 3g (5%); Total Fat 1.g (2%) (Sat. O.3g (2%)); Chol. 0mg (0%); Carb. 90g (30%); Fiber 7g (29%); Sugars 69g; Calcium 46mg (12%); Iron .87mg (5%); Sodium 15mg (1%); Vit. C 70mg (116%); Vit. A 1661 IU (33%); Trans fat 0g

# Fruit and Vegetable Smoothie

| Category: Creative | Prep and Cook Time: 10 minutes | Serves: 2 |
|---|---|---|

| Food Cost (per serving) | Restaurant Price | 1 Month Savings | 1 Year Savings |
|---|---|---|---|
| $1.50 | $4.00 | $10.00 | $120.00 |

Many people find that drinking their daily dose of fruits and vegetables is a palatable way to consume these vital foods. This smoothie is an excellent choice, especially when the fruits are in season.

**6 to 8 romaine lettuce leaves or other greens
(remove stems before putting in juicer or blender)
4 apricots, pitted and sliced
1 banana, peeled
1/4 cup blueberries (remove stems before putting
in juicer or blender)
2 cups water**

## Directions:

1. Put fruits and vegetables in a juicer or a blender.
2. Add 2 cups of water.
3. Mix on high speed.

**Nutritional information per serving (daily value):** Calories 193; Protein 4g (7%); Total Fat 1g (2%); (Sat. 0.2g (1%)); Chol 0mg (0%); Carb 48g (16%); Fiber 7g (27%); Sugars 31g; Calcium 41mg (4%); Iron .95mg (5%); Sodium 17mg (1%); Vit. C 28mg (46%); Vit. A 2791 IU (56%); Trans fat 0g

# Pear and Kale Smoothie

| Category: Creative | Prep and Cook Time: 15 minutes | Serves: 2 |
|---|---|---|
| **Food Cost (per serving)** | **Restaurant Price** | **1 Month Savings** | **1 Year Savings** |
| $1.50 | $4.00 | $10.00 | $120.00 |

Kale can be a difficult leafy vegetable to eat habitually, but in a smoothie it goes down easily and you do not even notice that it is "healthy." Kale is a good source of Vitamin K1, which is needed for bone and blood health. It also contains suloraphane, a chemical that prevents cancer cells from growing.

**2 pears, peeled and cored**
**2 kale leaves or other greens**
**mint (*optional*)**

## Directions:

1. Put fruits and vegetables in a juicer or a blender.
2. Add 2 cups of water.
3. Mix on high speed.

**Nutritional information per serving (daily value):** Calories 248; Protein 5g (10%); Total Fat 1g (2%) (Sat. 0.122g (1%)); Chol. 0mg (0%); Carb. 63g (21%); Fiber 13g (50%); Sugars 33g; Calcium 181mg (18%); Iron 2mg (14%); Sodium 51mg (2%); Vit. C 148mg (247%); Vit. A 17297 IU (346%); Trans fat 0g

# Yogurt Parfait

| Category: Creative | Prep and Cook Time: 15 minutes | Serves: 2 |
|---|---|---|

| Food Cost (per serving) | Restaurant Price | 1 Month Savings | 1 Year Savings |
|---|---|---|---|
| $2.00 | $5.50 | $14.00 | $168.00 |

Blueberries make delicious desserts, and a yogurt parfait is a perfect way to consume more of these fresh or frozen berries. The cost is calculated for blueberries in season.

**1 cup blueberries**
**2 cups plain or vanilla yogurt (low-fat)**
**1 tsp. honey or agave nectar**
**1/2 cup granola**

## Directions:

1. Layer in lunch container with fruit first, then yogurt, drizzled with 1/2 tsp honey or agave.
2. Top yogurt with granola and more honey to taste. Eat as is or continue to layer in the order listed.

**Nutritional information per serving (daily value):** Calories 410; Protein 17g (34%); Total Fat 11g (16%): Sat. 3g (16%)); Chol. 12mg (4%); Carb. 64g (21%); Fiber 5g (18%); Sugars 50g; Calcium 447mg (45%); Iron 2mg (9%); Sodium 170mg (7%); Vit. C 10mg (16%); Vit. A 151 IU (3%): Trans fat 0g

# Midday Gourmet Lunch Style

The Midday Gourmet person is willing to cook in the evenings or on the weekend to prepare lunch items for the upcoming week. With a little advanced preparation time, you can have lunch and leftovers for an entire week.

In this section, you will find easy-to-create recipes organized in six categories: main course entrées, spreads, soups, salads, sandwiches, and snacks. This is the section of the book with the most recipes because with some dedicated cooking for lunches, you will be bringing Midday Gourmet lunches with you daily and still saving money. Begin checking out the recipe websites on page 120 and begin expanding your lunch recipe collection. Once you begin to use the Midday Gourmet recipes regularly, you will begin to appreciate how easy it is to make a good, healthier lunch. Hopefully, you are also beginning to reap big savings.

Always refer to lunch suggestions in all the previous sections before completing your lunch menu. Think about how hungry you are at lunchtime and remember to add one to three Grab and Go items with your selection. Don't forget to add your Grab and Go items in your final lunch cost.

### Main Course Entrées

These entrées make great dinners and lunch leftovers. You may have to double the recipe depending on how many people you are feeding for dinner.

### Spreads

These two recipes can save you money if you like the hummus and pesto recipes found in the Almost Grab and Go section of the book. I added them here because if you are a true Grab and Go person, you need the spreads all ready to use in the morning when you are grabbing your lunch. Take a couple of minutes on the weekend or evening to create these recipes.

### Soups

These soups are easy to prepare and make great lunches. I can easily eat any of these recipes for at least two lunches during the following week. Each time I have the soup, it tastes even better than when I made it. You can also put portions of the soup in freezer containers to enjoy at a later date.

### Salads

These salads are all easy to prepare. When making the salad on the weekend, put in airtight container without salad dressing. Put the salad dressing in an additional small container and pour the dressing at lunchtime just before eating.

### Sandwiches

Here are a couple of sandwiches that take a little extra time to prepare but taste great for a weekday lunch if wrapped in an airtight container or tightly with sandwich wrap. Look at the sandwich selection in the other categories of the book, or check the websites on page 120 for additional ideas.

### Snacks

Here are a couple of quick items that can easily be added to your Grab and Go list. Make them on the weekend and enjoy the benefits throughout the week as mid-morning snacks or Grab and Go items.

# Midday Gourmet Recipes

# Homemade Vegetable Stew

| Category: Midday Gourmet | Prep and Cook Time: 45 minutes | Serves: 4 |
|---|---|---|

| Food Cost (per serving) | Restaurant Price | 1 Month Savings | 1 Year Savings |
|---|---|---|---|
| $1.50 | $8.00 | $26.00 | $312.00 |

Stew for lunch? This is absolutely a solid nutritional choice and a great way to use delicious leftovers.

1 tbsp. vegetable oil
1/2 cup onion, chopped
2 pieces of celery, chopped
2 carrots, cut in small pieces
1 large potato, cut in
    small pieces

1 zucchini, cut in small pieces
4 sprigs cilantro or parsley
1 can diced tomatoes (15 oz.)
1 tsp. vegetable broth
salt and pepper, to taste

## Directions:

1. Add oil to large pot and heat for about 1 minute
2. Add onions and celery and cook until tender.
3. Add the rest of the ingredients to the pot.
4. Cover and simmer slowly until vegetables are tender (about 30 minutes).

**Nutritional Information per serving (daily value):** Calories 142; Protein 4g (7%); Total Fat 4g (6%) (Sat. 37g (2%)); Chol. 0mg(0%); Carb. 25g (33%); Fiber 5g (22%); Sugars 7g; Calcium 71 mg (7%); Iron 1mg (8%); Sodium 153mg (6%); Vit. C 37mg (62%); Vit. A 6577 IU (132%); Trans Fat 0.01g

# Easy Spinach Lasagna

| Category: Midday Gourmet | Prep and Cook Time: 15 minutes | Serves: 8 |
|---|---|---|

| Food Cost (per serving) | Restaurant Price | 1 Month Savings | 1 Year Savings |
|---|---|---|---|
| $1.50 | $8.50 | $28.00 | $336.00 |

Spinach Lasagna is an excellent vegetarian alternative to the animal protein version. Give this recipe a good trial for your own taste test. Serve it for dinner and enjoy the leftovers for lunch.

**1 12 oz. pkg. frozen spinach, thawed**
**1 lb. firm tofu**
**1 tbsp. minced garlic**
**1 tsp. salt**
**10 small mushrooms, sliced (*optional*)**

**1 30 oz. jar pasta sauce**
**1 lb. lasagna noodles (cooked or use non-cook noodles)**
**1/4 cup grated Parmesan cheese or other hard cheese**

Preheat oven to 325 degrees.

## Directions:

1. Mix together spinach, garlic, firm tofu, and salt in a large mixing bowl.
2. Spread a thin layer of pasta sauce on the bottom of a 9x13 baking pan.
3. Add a layer of lasagna noodles, overlapping the noodles slightly (make sure you either cook the noodles or use non-cook noodles).
4. Add 1/2 of the spinach mix on top of the noodles.
5. Add another layer of lasagna noodles.
6. Add a layer of pasta sauce to cover the noodles.
7. Add a layer of mushrooms (*optional*).
8. Repeat a layer of noodles, pasta sauce, spinach mix, and mushrooms. Then repeat layers until you reach the top of the pan.
9. Spread Parmesan cheese on top.
10. Cover top tightly with aluminum foil and bake for 60 minutes.

---

**Nutritional information per serving (daily value):** Calories 263; Protein 13g (26%); Total Fat 13g (20%) (Sat. 6g (29%)); Chol. 25mg (8%); Carb. 24g (8%); Fiber 4g (15%); Sugars 3g; Calcium 279mg (28%); Iron 2mg (12%); Sodium 371mg (15%); Vit. C 12mg (20%); Vit. A 2523 IU (50%); Trans fat 0g

# Cooking a Whole Chicken

| Category: Midday Gourmet | Prep and Cook Time: 80 minutes | Serves: 6 |
|---|---|---|

| Food Cost (per serving) | Restaurant Price | 1 Month Savings | 1 Year Savings |
|---|---|---|---|
| $1.50 | $7.50 | $24.00 | $288.00 |

Roasted chicken is an excellent source of protein, but try to purchase those that are organically fed and free-range. Chicken is the most economical when you buy it whole, although I must admit when creating many of the cooked chicken recipes, I buy a cooked rotisserie chicken at the grocery store.

**One 3.5 lb. chicken placed on a baking pan or aluminum foil (if you buy a larger chicken, add 8-10 minutes per pound for cooking time)**

**salt and pepper**
**3 tbsp. butter or margarine**
**1/2 cup carrots, cut in small pieces**
**2 potatoes, cut in small pieces**
**1/2 onion, cut in small pieces**

Preheat oven to 325 degrees.

## Directions:

1. Take the chicken out of its packaging and remove the giblets from the inside of the chicken. You may want to use plastic gloves when you do this. Rinse bird thoroughly and dry with a paper towel.
2. Cover the chicken with salt and pepper and spread 3 tbsp. of butter all over the chicken using a piece of paper towel or your hand. And put some of the butter on the bottom of the baking pan or aluminum foil. Place chicken breast side up.
3. After the chicken has baked about 20 minutes, add the carrots, potatoes, and onion and 1 cup of water to the pan.
4. Cook another 45 minutes. (For anything over 3.5 pounds, add about 8-10 minutes per pound.)

**Nutritional information per serving (daily value):** Calories 263; Protein 13g (26%); Total Fat 13g (20%) (Sat. 6g (29%)); Chol. 25mg (8%); Carb. 24g (8%); Fiber 4g (15%); Sugars 3g; Calcium 279mg (28%); Iron 2mg (12%); Sodium 371mg (15%); Vit. C 12mg (20%); Vit. A 2523 IU (50%); Trans fat 0g

# Homemade Chili

| Category: Midday Gourmet | | Prep and Cook Time: 30 minutes | Serves: 4 |
|---|---|---|---|

| Food Cost (per serving) | Restaurant Price | 1 Month Savings | 1 Year Savings |
|---|---|---|---|
| $2.00 | $6.50 | $18.00 | $192.00 |

This is a hearty protein dish that relies on beans to provide part of the total protein content. It is an excellent dinner and leftover lunch for folks of all ages even without the beef.

**1 lb. ground beef**
**1 onion, chopped**
**1 (14.5 oz.) can stewed tomatoes**
**1 (15 oz.) can tomato sauce**
**1 (15 oz.) can kidney beans**
**1-1/2 cups water**

**1 pinch chili powder (add more if you like hot chili)**
**1 pinch garlic powder**
**salt and pepper, to taste**
**shredded cheese (*optional*)**

## Directions:

1. In a large pot, sauté until meat is browned and onion is tender. Remove and drain meat on a paper towel. Return drained meat and onion to pot.
2. Add the stewed tomatoes with juice, tomato sauce, beans, and water.
3. Season with the chili powder, garlic powder, salt and ground pepper to taste.
4. Bring to a boil; reduce heat to low.
5. Cover and let simmer for at least 15 minutes.
6. Sprinkle with shredded cheese (*optional*).

**Nutritional information per serving (daily value) – without cheese:** Calories 362; Protein 31g (62%); Total Fat 12g (19%) (Sat. 5g (24%)); Chol. 73mg (24%); Carb. 33g (11%); Fiber 9g (35%); Sugars 11g; Calcium 99mg (10%); Iron 7mg (39%); Sodium 1342mg (56%); Vit. C 21mg (35%); Vit A 973 IU (19%); Trans fat 0.72g

# Homemade Vegetarian Chili

| Category: | Midday Gourmet | | Prep and Cook Time: | 30 minutes | Serves: | 4 |
|---|---|---|---|---|---|---|

| Food Cost (per serving) | Restaurant Price | 1 Month Savings | 1 Year Savings |
|---|---|---|---|
| $1.50 | $5.50 | $16.00 | $192.00 |

This is a nutritious, tasty recipe that will be enjoyed by non-vegetarians too. Only 263 calories and a great choice for a cold winter's night.

**2 tbsp. olive oil**
**1 onion, chopped**
**1 (14.5 oz.) can stewed tomatoes**
**1 (15 oz.) can tomato sauce**
**1 (15 oz.) can kidney beans**
**1-1/2 cups water**

**1 pinch chili powder (add more**
 **if you like hot chili)**
**1 pinch garlic powder**
**salt and pepper, to taste**
**shredded cheese (*optional*)**

## Directions:

1. Sauté onion in a large pot with olive oil until tender
2. Add the stewed tomatoes with juice, tomato sauce, beans, and water.
3. Season with the chili powder, garlic powder, salt and pepper to taste.
4. Bring to a boil; reduce heat to low.
5. Cover and let simmer for at least 15 minutes.
6. Sprinkle with shredded cheese (*optional*).

**Nutritional information per serving (daily value):** Calories 263; Protein 13g (26%); Total Fat 13g (20%) (Sat. 6g (29%)); Chol. 25mg (8%); Carb. 24g (8%); Fiber 4g (15%); Sugars 3g; Calcium 279mg (28%); Iron 2mg (12%); Sodium 371mg (15%); Vit. C 12mg (20%); Vit. A 2523 IU (50%); Trans fat 0g

# Homemade Meatballs

| Category: Midday Gourmet | Prep and Cook Time: 30 minutes | Serves: 6 |
|---|---|---|

| Food Cost (per serving) | Restaurant Price | 1 Month Savings | 1 Year Savings |
|---|---|---|---|
| $1.00* | $5.50 | $18.00 | $216.00 |

Meatballs are a high-protein dish that comes at a relatively low cost per serving. There is definitely a satisfaction that comes from forming meatballs and knowing exactly what the ingredients are rather than opening a package. When ready to eat, mix and heat with pasta sauce, add pasta, and have a delicious spaghetti and meatballs dinner. Or you can make six sandwiches.

**1 egg**
**2 tbsp. water**
**1/2 cup packaged breadcrumbs**
**1/4 cup minced onion**

**1/2 tsp. salt**
**1/8 tsp. pepper**
**1 lb. lean ground beef**

Preheat oven to 350 degrees.

## Directions:

1. In large bowl, combine egg, water, breadcrumbs, onion, salt, and pepper.
2. Add ground beef, broken into chunks, and mush with your hands to combine. Form into meatballs about 1" in diameter and place on a baking pan.
3. Bake in a large pan at 350 degrees for 25-30 minutes until meatballs are no longer pink in center. Cool and freeze some for future lunches.

*Adding the cost of bread, lettuce, and tomato for the sandwich option, each sandwich will cost approximately $1.50.

**Nutritional information per serving (daily value):** Calories 153; Protein 18g (37%); Total Fat 5g (8%) (Sat. 2g (10%)); Chol. 82mg (27%); Carb. 7g (2%); Fiber 1g (2%); Sugars 1g; Calcium 30mg (3%); Iron 2mg (13%); Sodium 324mg (13%); Vit. C .50mg (1%); Vit. A 41 IU (1%); Trans fat 0.25g

# Beef and Tomato Stew

| Category: Midday Gourmet | | Prep and Cook Time: 80 minutes | | Serves: 6 |
|---|---|---|---|---|

| Food Cost (per serving) | Restaurant Price | 1 Month Savings | 1 Year Savings |
|---|---|---|---|
| $2.50 | $8.00 | $22.00 | $264.00 |

Stew is tasty, hearty, and nutritious; it is a good choice when a heavy lunch and light dinner are desired. This is a great recipe for dinner for two and leftovers for two to four lunches.

2 tsp. olive oil
2 lbs. steak, trimmed of fat
   and cut into 1/2-inch pieces
1/2 medium onion, cut in
   small pieces
3 cloves garlic, minced
2 cups vegetable broth (or
   vegetable broth granules
   and water as stated on the package)

1 lb. potatoes, cut in small pieces
2 cups sliced carrots
1 (28 oz.) can crushed tomatoes
   or 25 oz. marinara sauce
1/2 cup chopped parsley or cilantro
salt and pepper, to taste

## Directions:

1. Heat oil in a 6-qt pot over medium heat.
2. Add beef; cook 5 minutes or until browned, stirring frequently.
3. Remove beef from pan, place on paper towel on a plate, reserving 1 tablespoon of drippings in pan.
4. Add onion and garlic; sauté 2 minutes or until onion begins to brown.
5. Add broth and bring to a boil.
6. Return meat to pan, add potatoes, carrots, crushed tomatoes or sauce, cilantro or parsley, and cook over low heat until it simmers (bubbling gently).
7. Cover and cook for 1 hour. If meat is not tender, let it simmer longer and check every 5 minutes. Add salt and pepper, to taste.

**Nutritional information per serving (daily value):** Calories 550; Protein 43g (86%); Total Fat 8g (13%) (Sat. 3g (12%)); Chol. 82mg (27%); Carb. 77g (26%); Fiber 13g (51%); Sugars 11g; Calcium 135mg (14%); Iron 7mg (38%); Sodium 332mg (14%); Vit. C 104 mg (174%); Vit. A 6733 IU (135%); Trans fat 0g

# Roast Beef for Sandwiches

| Category: Midday Gourmet | Prep and Cook Time: 3-4.25 hours | Serves: 4 |
|---|---|---|

| Food Cost (per serving) | Restaurant Price | 1 Month Savings | 1 Year Savings |
|---|---|---|---|
| $2.50 | $8.00 | $22.00 | $264.00 |

Roast beef makes a tasty lunch but vary this protein with fruits and vegetables. I often add lettuce and tomato to make this sandwich even more scrumptious.

**3 lb. chuck roast (wash and dry roast with paper towels)**
**1 large onion, cut in small pieces**
**3 or 4 beef bouillon cubes**

**1/2 tsp. garlic powder**
**salt and pepper, to taste**
**4 Kaiser rolls**

Preheat oven to 325 degrees.

## Directions:

1. Put 1 1/2 inches of water in bottom of large oven pan. Then add onion, beef bouillon cubes, garlic powder, and mix.
2. Add roast to the pan and sprinkle salt and pepper on top.
3. Cover and bake for 3 hours. If you don't have a lid, use aluminum foil and cover tightly.
4. At about 3 hours baking time, remove roast. Cut fat off meat and remove bones. Cut meat into small pieces, and taste. If it is not done, return for 15 minutes and taste again. Keep checking after 5 minutes to make sure it doesn't get too dry.
5. Serve in juices or with your favorite meat sauce on rolls.

**Nutritional information per serving (daily value):** Calories: 889; Protein 61g (122%); Total Fat 68g (173%); (Sat. 46g (1057%)); Chol. 241mg (81%); Carb. 4g (1%); Fiber .68g (3%); Sugars 2g; Calcium 60mg (6%); Iron 7mg (41%); Sodium 1181 mg (49%); Vit. C 3mg (5%); Vit. A .75 IU (0%); Trans fat 0g

# 15-Minute Hummus

| Category: | Midday Gourmet | Prep and Cook Time: | 15 minutes | Serves: | 4 |
|---|---|---|---|---|---|

| Food Cost (per serving) | Restaurant Price | 1 Month Savings | 1 Year Savings |
|---|---|---|---|
| $0.50 | $2.50 | $8.00 | $96.00 |

Hummus is easy to prepare and is so nutritious that it should be a regular addition for healthy lunches. If you have the time to make your own hummus, you can see how easy it is and how much you save from buying it already made. You will know the ingredients you are eating and can save even more money when preparing the Hummus Salad Wrap on page 21 or bring crackers for a great Grab and Go lunch.

**1 (15 oz.) can garbanzo beans, drained; reserve liquid**
**1 garlic clove cut up**
**1 tsp. salt**
**1/2 tsp. pepper**
**1 tbsp. olive oil**
**2 tsp. ground cumin**

## Directions:

1. Combine all ingredients in a blender or food processor. Blend on low speed.
2. Add some of the reserved liquid if you want thinner hummus.

**Nutritional information per serving (daily value):** Calories 125; Protein 5g (11%); Total Fat 4g (7%) (Sat. 6g (3%); Chol. 0mg (0%); Carb. 17g (6%); Fiber 5g (20%); Sugars .2g, Calcium 56mg (6%); Iron 2mg (13%); Sodium 900mg (38%); Vit. C 1mg (2%); Vit. A 13 IU (0%); Trans fat 0g

# 15-Minute Pesto*

| Category: | Midday Gourmet | Prep and Cook Time: | 20 minutes | Serves: | 4 |
|-----------|----------------|---------------------|------------|---------|---|

| Food Cost (per serving) | Restaurant Price | 1 Month Savings | 1 Year Savings |
|-------------------------|------------------|-----------------|----------------|
| $1.00 | $2.50* | $6.00 | $72.00 |

Pesto is a healthy and tasty addition to many recipes, so it is wise to keep a jar in your refrigerator for fast lunch preparation. You can save if you make your own pesto for the Pesto and Tomato Sandwich and Provolone-Pesto Wrap found on pages 23 and 49.

**2 tbsp. chopped almonds**
**1 cup fresh basil leaves**
**2 cloves garlic, cut up**
**1/3 cup olive oil**
**pinch of ground nutmeg (*optional*)**

Preheat oven or toaster oven to 325 degrees.

## Directions:

1. Place almonds on a cookie sheet in the oven for for 10 minutes or until lightly toasted.
2. In a blender or food processor, combine all of the ingredients and mix at low speed until spreadable paste forms.
3. Store in airtight container.

* Usually served in a restaurant with pasta or sandwiches.

**Nutritional information per serving (daily value):** Calories 155; Protein 2g (5%); Total Fat 16g (24%) (Sat. 2g (10%)); Chol. 0mg (0%); Carb. 3 (1%); Fiber 1g (5%); Sugars .28g; Calcium 110mg (11%); Iron 2mg (11%); Sodium 3mg (0%); Vit. C 11mg (18%); Vit. A 2954 IU (59%); Trans fat 0g

# Grandma's Chicken Soup

| Category: Midday Gourmet | Prep and Cook Time: 30 minutes | Serves: 6 |
|---|---|---|

| Food Cost (per serving) | Restaurant Price | 1 Month Savings | 1 Year Savings |
|---|---|---|---|
| $2.00 | $6.00 | $16.00 | $192.00 |

There is a reason that chicken soup remains a favorite to ward off colds. This recipe has been a real favorite for people of all ages. Buying a cooked chicken in the deli section of the supermarket works well in this recipe if you don't have time to bake the chicken. Be careful in your sources of chicken and chicken broth. Organic is best.

**32 oz. vegetable or chicken broth
  (can use broth granules and water)
4 cups cooked chicken
1 cup celery, chopped
1 cup carrots, chopped
1/2 cup onion, chopped
1 (15 oz.) can creamed corn
1/2 cup pasta sauce**

## Directions:

1. Add 4 cups of cooked chicken and broth to large pot.
2. Add rest of the ingredients and stir.
3. Cook approximately 30 minutes or until vegetables are tender.

**Nutritional information per serving (daily value):** Calories 233; Protein 17g (36%); Total Fat 5g (8%) (Sat. 1g (6%)); Chol. 42mg (14%); Carb. 30g (10%); Fiber 3g (30%); Sugars 5g; Calcium 42mg (4%); Iron 2mg (11%); Sodium 1006mg (42%); Vit. C 17mg (29%); Vit. A 2684 IU (54%); Trans fat 0g

# Fresh Vegetable Soup

| Category: Midday Gourmet | Prep and Cook Time: 45 minutes | Serves: 6 |
|---|---|---|

| Food Cost (per serving) | Restaurant Price | 1 Month Savings | 1 Year Savings |
|---|---|---|---|
| $1.00 | $5.00 | $16.00 | $192.00 |

Soup is a very palatable way to increase your vegetable consumption. Have it for dinner and then enjoy the leftovers for lunch. Add water the next day if soup appears dry.

**1 tbsp. olive oil**
**1/2 cup onion, cut in small pieces**
**1 cup carrots, cut in small pieces**
**2 medium potatoes, cut in small pieces**
**1 cup green beans, cut in small pieces**

**1 tbsp. cilantro or parsley**
**32 oz. vegetable broth**
  **or use vegetable broth granules**
**salt and pepper to taste**
**Add other favorite**
  **spices or herbs (*optional*)**

## Directions:

1. Add oil to large pot and heat for about 1 minute.
2. Add onions and celery and cook until tender.
3. Add the rest of the ingredients to pot and bring to boil.
4. Cover and simmer slowly until vegetables are tender (about 30 minutes).

**Nutritional information per serving (daily value):** Calories 186; Protein 8g (15%); Total Fat 3g (4%) (Sat. .4g (2%); Chol. 0mg (0%); Carb. 32g (11%); Fiber 8g (31%); Sugars 4g; Calcium 36mg (4%); Iron 2.7mg (15%); Sodium 14mg (1%); Vit. C 15mg (25%); Vit. A 3200 IU (64%); Trans fat 0g

# Tomato and Basil Soup

| Category: Midday Gourmet | Prep and Cook Time: 20 minutes | Serves: 4 |
|---|---|---|

| Food Cost (per serving) | Restaurant Price | 1 Month Savings | 1 Year Savings |
|---|---|---|---|
| $1.50 | $5.50 | $16.00 | $192.00 |

Creamy tomato soup is a childhood comfort food that carries its "warm-in-the-tummy" feeling into adult lunches. One cup of creamy tomato soup provides 55 percent of your daily-recommended value of vitamin C and 79 percent of vitamin A. Basil is an aromatic herb that adds vitamins A and K to the soup.

**2 tbsp. olive or vegetable oil**
**2 lb. Roma tomatoes, cut in small pieces**
**1/2 cup fresh basil leaves**
**1/2 cup vegetable broth or granules and water**
**1/2 cup heavy cream (or use milk)**
**salt and pepper to taste**

## Directions:

1. Heat oil in 3-4 qt. pot over medium heat. Add tomatoes and 1/4 cup basil leaves. Cook, stirring often, until tomatoes are soft (10-15 minutes).
2. Transfer to blender or food processor and add broth and cream. Whirl until smooth and season with salt and pepper.
3. Add 1/4 cup of basil leaves on top of soup for individual servings. Serve hot or cold.

**Nutritional information per serving (daily value):** Calories 166; Protein 4g (8%), Total Fat 13g (19%) (Sat. 7g (36%)); Chol. 41mg (14%); Carb. 12g (1%); Fiber 3g (13%); Sugars 6g; Calcium 86mg (9%); Iron 2mg (9%); Sodium 191mg (8%); Vit. C 33 mg (55%); Vit. A 3940 IU (79%); Trans fat 0g

# Chicken Tortilla Soup

| Category: Midday Gourmet | Prep and Cook Time: 4 hours | Serves: 6 |
|---|---|---|

| Food Cost (per serving) | Restaurant Price | 1 Month Savings | 1 Year Savings |
|---|---|---|---|
| $2.50 | $7.00 | $18.00 | $216.00 |

Chicken and beans are both good sources of protein. This is a great recipe to bring to a potluck dinner and hopefully have leftovers for lunch. Before serving this recipe to company, you may want to take out your lunch portion because it is a favorite for all ages.

**3 cups uncooked boneless chicken pieces**
**2 (13 oz.) cans black beans with liquid**
**2 (15 oz.) cans stewed tomatoes with liquid**
**1 cup mild or medium salsa**
**1 (15 oz.) can tomato sauce**
**1 large bag of corn chips**

## Directions:

1. Stir the first five ingredients into a large pot with lid or crock-pot and cook on low heat for 3-4 hours or until chicken is done. Stir and taste-test the chicken to make sure it is ready to eat.
2. When chicken is done, take out of pot and cut in small pieces and then put back in pot.
3. To serve, crush tortilla chips in bottom of soup bowl, then pour soup on top of chips.

*Optional:* Add 4 oz. sour cream and/or 1/4 lb. shredded Monterey Jack or Cheddar cheese to each bowl when serving.

**Nutritional information per serving (daily value):** Calories 329; Protein 12g (24%); Total Fat 11g (16%); (Sat. 1.45g (7%)); Chol. 2mg (1%); Carb. 50g (17%); Fiber 11g (45%); Sugars 10g; Calcium 160mg (16%); Iron 4mg (23%); Sodium 1391mg (58%); Vit. C 20mg (34%); Vit. A 595 IU (12%); Trans fat 0g

# Vegetarian Corn Chowder

| Category: Midday Gourmet | Prep and Cook Time: 35 minutes | Serves: 4 |
|---|---|---|

| Food Cost (per serving) | Restaurant Price | 1 Month Savings | 1 Year Savings |
|---|---|---|---|
| $1.50 | $4.50 | $12.00 | $144.00 |

Corn seems to be a year-round favorite because it cans and freezes well. It is a good source of phosphorus, magnesium, manganese, iron, and selenium. It is also a good source of B vitamins. Add a small salad and a piece of fruit and your lunch is complete.

**4 tbsp. margarine or butter**
**2 tbsp. onion, chopped**
**1/3 cup celery, chopped**
**1/4 cup all-purpose flour**
**1 (14.5 oz.) can vegetable broth or vegetable granules and water**
**1 can (15 oz.) creamed corn**
**1 (15 oz.) can whole-kernel corn, drained**
**1 tbsp. sliced carrots**
**2/3 cup half-and-half or skim milk**
**salt and pepper, to taste**

## Directions:

1. In a large saucepan over medium heat, melt margarine or butter.
2. Cook onions and celery in butter for 3 minutes.
3. Mix and stir in flour and cook 6 minutes more, until light brown.
4. Mix in broth and simmer 10 minutes.
5. Stir in canned creamed corn, whole-kernel corn, carrot, half-and-half or milk, pepper and salt, and simmer over low heat 10 minutes more. Make sure it is on low heat and does not boil.

**Nutritional information per serving (daily value):** Calories 298; Protein 6g (12%); Total Fat 18 (27%) (Sat. 5g (25%)); Chol. 15mg (5%); Carb. 35g (14%); Fiber 4g (16%); Sugars 5g; Calcium 57mg (6%); Iron 2mg (9%); Sodium 716mg (30%); Vit. C 16mg (26%); Vit. A 936 IU (19%); Trans fat 0g

# Vegetarian Minestrone Soup

| Category: Midday Gourmet | Prep and Cook Time: 45 minutes | Serves: 6 |
|---|---|---|

| Food Cost (per serving) | Restaurant Price | 1 Month Savings | 1 Year Savings |
|---|---|---|---|
| $1.50 | $6.00 | $18.00 | $216.00 |

Vegetarian soup is an excellent way to enjoy vegetables while reaping their vitamin and mineral nutritional benefits. This is an easy vegetable soup that the entire family will enjoy.

**12 oz. jar of pasta sauce (tomato and basil works well)**
**12 oz. water**
**8 oz. vegetable broth**
**1 lb. frozen Italian vegetables**
**1/8 tsp. garlic salt**
**1 tsp. sugar**
**1 tsp. oregano**
**salt and pepper, to taste**
**1/2 cup small pasta (elbow macaroni or small penne)**
**6 tbsp. Parmesan cheese**

## Directions:

1. Put first seven ingredients in a large pot.
2. Bring to a boil, cover, turn the heat to low, and simmer for 15 minutes. Taste vegetables and add more time at 5-minute intervals if vegetables are not tender.
3. Cook pasta in a separate pot according to package directions. (Taste to make sure pasta is done.)
4. Put pasta in soup bowl when done, and add soup.
5. Sprinkle Parmesan cheese over soup when ready to eat. Serve for dinner and then put leftovers in small containers.

**Nutritional information per serving (daily value):** Calories 116; Protein 7g (13%); Total Fat 3g (4%) (Sat. 1g (7%)); Chol. 6mg (2%); Carb. 17g (6%); Fiber .3g (13%); Sugars 1g; Calcium 122mg (12%); Iron 0.95mg (5%); Sodium 170mg (7%); Vit. C 8g (13%); Vit. A 3 860 IU(77%); Trans fat 0g

# Fresh Carrot Soup

| Category: Midday Gourmet | Prep and Cook Time: 30 minutes | Serves: 4 |
|---|---|---|

| Food Cost (per serving) | Restaurant Price | 1 Month Savings | 1 Year Savings |
|---|---|---|---|
| $1.00 | $4.50 | $14.00 | $168.00 |

Carrots are low in saturated fat and cholesterol and high in dietary fiber, vitamin A, vitamin C, and calcium. This soup is so tasty and easy to make. If you are making it for folks who don't like celery or carrots, mix in blender before serving to disguise the celery and carrots.

2 tbsp. olive oil
1/2 onion, chopped
2 cloves garlic, chopped
1 tsp. curry powder (add more
   if you like spicy food)

4 cups vegetable broth or use
   vegetable broth granules and water
5 large fresh carrots, chopped
5 stalks celery, chopped
salt and pepper, to taste

## Directions:

1. Heat olive oil in pot and fry onion and garlic until tender (about 5 minutes).
2. Add curry powder.
3. Add all other ingredients and cook until carrot and celery pieces are tender (about 20 minutes).
4. Add salt and pepper, to taste.

*Optional:* Blend in food processor or blender until vegetables are not obvious. Top with yogurt or sour cream.

**Nutritional information per serving (daily value):** Calories 122; Protein 4g (7%); Total Fat 1g (2%) (Sat. 0.2g (1%)); Chol. 0mg (0%); Carb. 26g (12%); Fiber 10g (39%); Sugars 14g; Calcium 176mg (18%); Iron 1mg (8%); Sodium 349mg (15%); Vit. C 19mg (32%); Vit. A 7835 IU (15%); Trans fat 0g

# Fresh Salmon and Spinach Salad

| Category: Midday Gourmet | Prep and Cook Time: 20 minutes | Serves: 4 |
|---|---|---|

| Food Cost (per serving) | Restaurant Price | 1 Month Savings | 1 Year Savings |
|---|---|---|---|
| $3.50 | $8.50 | $20.00 | $240.00 |

One 4-ounce serving of salmon is a good source of protein and omega-3 fatty acids. Combine this with vitamins and minerals from spinach for a healthy taste treat. An elegant lunch when you want to treat yourself to something special.

1 lb. salmon
salt and pepper
10 oz. washed spinach
1/2 pint small tomatoes, halved and washed

1/3 cup Feta cheese, crumbled
1/4 cup almond pieces
1/4 cup balsamic oil and vinegar dressing

## Directions:

1. Heat broiler, setting rack 4 inches from heat.
2. Place salmon skin side down on a foil-lined rimmed baking sheet; season with salt and pepper.
3. Broil, without turning, until opaque throughout, about 7 to 9 minutes or until the fish reaches desired doneness. Let cool briefly.
4. Place spinach and tomatoes in bowl. Top with salmon, Feta cheese, and almonds.
5. Pour bottled or homemade oil and vinegar dressing on top before ready to eat.

**Nutritional information per serving (daily value):** Calories 367; Protein 28g (55%); Total Fat 27g (41%) (Sat. 4g (21%)); Chol. 73mg (24%); Carb. 4g (1%); Fiber 2g (9%); Sugars 1g; Calcium 163mg (16%); Iron 3mg (17%); Sodium 244mg (10%); Vit. C 23mg (39%); Vit. A 6898 IU (138%); Trans fat 0.055g

# Pasta Salad with Black Beans and Spinach

| Category: Midday Gourmet | Prep and Cook Time: 25 minutes | Serves: 4 |
|---|---|---|

| Food Cost (per serving) | Restaurant Price | 1 Month Savings | 1 Year Savings |
|---|---|---|---|
| $1.50 | $7.50 | $24.00 | $288.00 |

Black beans are a good source of cholesterol-lowering fiber. The high fiber content prevents blood sugar levels from rising too rapidly after a meal, making these beans an especially good choice for individuals with diabetes, insulin resistance, or hypoglycemia (low blood sugar). The addition of fresh greens makes this a powerhouse lunch.

**8 oz. penne or other small pasta**
**1/3 cup vegetable or olive oil**
**1 tbsp. garlic, chopped**
**12 oz. frozen spinach or fresh greens (about 6 cups)**
**1 can (15 oz) diced tomatoes with liquid**
**1 can (15 oz) black beans, drained**
**1/2 cup shredded Parmesan cheese**
**salt and pepper to taste**

## Directions:

1. Cook pasta according to directions.
2. Heat oil in large pot. Add garlic and cook on low until it is soft.
3. Add next three ingredients.
4. When mixture begins to bubble, cook uncovered for about 5 minutes.
5. Add pasta and Parmesan cheese to vegetable mixture, and toss.

**Nutritional information per serving (daily value):** Calories 563; Protein 23g (45%); Total Fat 24g (38%) (Sat. 6g (28%)); Chol. 11mg (4%); Carb. 65g (43%); Fiber 11g (26%); Sugars 7g; Calcium 389mg (39%); Iron 5mg (27%); Sodium 2564mg (107%); Vit. C 16mg (26%); Vit. A 10103 IU (202%); Trans fat 0g

# Fresh Fruit Salad

| Category: Midday Gourmet | Prep and Cook Time: 20 minutes | Serves: 4 |
|---|---|---|

| Food Cost (per serving) | Restaurant Price | 1 Month Savings | 1 Year Savings |
|---|---|---|---|
| *$2.00 | $7.00 | $20.00 | $240.00 |

The important nutrients in fresh fruit salad include vitamins A and C as well as potassium, calcium, iron, vitamin E, vitamin K, thiamin, riboflavin, vitamin B6, phosphorus, and zinc. I have tried this salad with many different fruits, and it has always been great, so shop for your favorites and watch for fruits that are in season.

*In-season prices

**2 bananas, peeled and sliced**
**1/2 lb. strawberries, rinsed, hulled, and sliced**
**1/4 lb. seedless green grapes**
**1/4 lb. seedless red grapes**
**3 peaches, peeled, pitted, and chopped**
***Dressing:* 1/4 cup pineapple juice,**
        **plus juice of one lime**

## Directions:

1. Combine chopped and sliced fruits in a large serving bowl and toss gently.
2. Mix together remaining ingredients in a small bowl.
3. Pour dressing mixture over fruit, and toss gently to combine. Cover bowl with aluminum foil and chill the fruit salad thoroughly before serving.

*Optional:* Serve over greens.

**Nutritional information per serving (daily value):** Calories 160; Protein 2g (5%); Total Fat 0.75g (1%) (Sat. 13g (1%); Chol. 0mg (0%); Carb. 40g (13%); Fiber 5g (19%); Sugars 29g; Calcium 26mg (3%); Iron .91mg (5%); Sodium 3mg (0%); Vit. C 53g (88%); Vit. A 442 IU (9%); Trans fat 0g

# Greek Tofu Salad

| Category: Midday Gourmet | Prep and Cook Time: 20 minutes | Serves: 4 |
|---|---|---|

| Food Cost (per serving) | Restaurant Price | 1 Month Savings | 1 Year Savings |
|---|---|---|---|
| $2.00 | $7.00 | $20.00 | $240.00 |

Tofu is a good source of protein that is relatively low in fat. One of the joys of tofu is that it takes on the flavors of whatever it is combined with. Expect Greek tofu salad to pick up flavors of Feta cheese and olives. If you like Greek salads, this makes an easy, tasty lunch.

**1/3 cup crumbled Feta cheese**
**1/4 cup red onion or scallions, chopped**
**12 green or black olives, pitted and cut in half**
**3 tbsp. lemon juice**
**1 tbsp. olive oil**
**8 oz. firm tofu, drained and cut up in small pieces**
**1 tomato, chopped**
**1 small cucumber, chopped (peel if waxed)**
**2 tbsp. chopped fresh parsley**
**salt and pepper, to taste**

## Directions:

1. Stir together Feta cheese, onion, olives, lemon juice, and oil in a medium bowl.
2. Add tofu and mix together with a fork.
3. Cover and refrigerate for at least 10 minutes.
4. Add tomato, cucumber, and parsley to tofu mixture.
5. salt and pepper, to taste.

**Nutritional information per serving (daily value):** Calories 137; Protein 7g (15%); Total Fat 8g (12%) (Sat. 3g (13%)); Chol. 11mg (4%); Carb. 11g (4%); Fiber 2g (8%); Sugars 5g; Calcium 145mg (15%); Iron 3mg (16%); Sodium 181mg (8%); Vit. C 45mg (75%); Vit. A 2571 IU (51%); Trans fat 0g

# Eggplant Parmesan Sandwich

| Category: Midday Gourmet | Prep and Cook Time: 20 minutes | Serves: 4 |
|---|---|---|

| Food Cost (per serving) | Restaurant Price | 1 Month Savings | 1 Year Savings |
|---|---|---|---|
| $2.00 | $5.50 | $14.00 | $168.00 |

Eggplant is low in saturated fat, sodium, and cholesterol; it is high in dietary fiber, folate, potassium, manganese, vitamin C, vitamin K, thiamin, niacin, vitamin B6, pantothenic acid, magnesium, phosphorus, and copper. It is like taking a multiple vitamin/mineral tablet, and is scrumptious to eat.

**2 tbsp. olive oil**
**1 large eggplant cut into approximately 1˝-thick slices**
**salt and pepper to taste**

**4 tomatoes, thinly sliced**
**4 sandwich rolls, split in half**
**1/2 cup shredded Parmesan cheese**
**1 bunch fresh basil**

## Directions:

1. Brush both sides of eggplant slices with olive oil, and season with salt and pepper in a large frying pan.
2. Fry eggplant on both sides about 3 minutes a side until soft.
3. Add Parmesan cheese to the top of the eggplant slices for a couple of minutes on each side.
4. Add the tomatoes to the pan for 2 minutes or until soft.
5. Put eggplant, several basil leaves, and tomato on sandwich roll. You may want to heat the sandwich before eating.

**Nutritional information per serving (daily value):** Calories 163 cal; Protein 8g (16%); Total Fat 11g (17%) (Sat. 4g (19%)); Chol. 11mg (4%); Carb. 9g (3%); Fiber 5g (20%); Sugars 3g; Calcium 248mg (25%); Iron 1mg (7%); Sodium 272mg (11%); Vit. C 794mg (11%); Vit. A 1275 IU (26%); Trans fat 0g

# Ham, Cheese and Asparagus Sandwich

| Category: Midday Gourmet | Prep and Cook Time: 20 minutes | Serves: 2 |
|---|---|---|

| Food Cost (per serving) | Restaurant Price | 1 Month Savings | 1 Year Savings |
|---|---|---|---|
| $3.50 | $7.50 | $16.00 | $192.00 |

This delicious combination sandwich is not for every day but for special treats and a clever way to use leftovers. The addition of asparagus adds green nutrients to the meal.

1/2 lb. fresh asparagus
3 tbsp. softened butter or margarine
1 small garlic clove, chopped
2 6-inch French bread loaves, split
3 tbsp. mayonnaise

4 baked ham slices
4 Swiss cheese slices
1/2 cup green leaf lettuce
2 plum tomatoes, thinly sliced

## Directions:

1. Break off tough ends of asparagus. Cook in boiling water to cover for 3 minutes or until crispy tender. Drain in strainer and put into ice water.
2. While asparagus is cooking and cooling, mix together butter and garlic and spread on bottom halves of bread.
3. Spread mayonnaise over the top halves of the bread.
4. Layer bottom halves with ham slices, asparagus, and cheese.
5. Place on cookie sheet and broil 2 inches from heat for 1 minute or just until cheese melts.
6. When ready to eat, top with lettuce, tomato, and top half of bread.

Sandwich is also great cool if you don't have a place to do step 5.

**Nutritional information per serving (daily value):** Calories 563; Protein 42g (84%); Total Fat 36g (56%) (Sat. 14g (71%)); Chol. 119mg (40%); Carb. 20g (7%); Fiber 6g (26%); Sugars 8g; Calcium 525mg (53%); Iron 6mg (36%); Sodium 1633mg (68%); Vit. C 32mg (53%); Vit. A 4562 IU (91%); Trans fat 0g

# Veggie Cream Cheese Squares

| Category: Midday Gourmet | Prep and Cook Time: 30 minutes | Serves: 4 |
|---|---|---|

| Food Cost (per serving) | Restaurant Price | 1 Month Savings | 1 Year Savings |
|---|---|---|---|
| $2.00 | $5.00 | $12.00 | $144.00 |

Veggie Cream Cheese Squares will give you bonus points as a gourmet cook. Zucchinis provide folate, potassium, and vitamins A and C. Zucchinis are also an excellent source of vitamin C. Green bell peppers provide vitamins A, C, and K. Add some fresh fruit to round out the lunch.

**1 (8 oz.) package refrigerated crescent rolls**
**1 (8 oz.) package cream cheese, softened**
**1 (1 oz.) package of dry ranch dressing**
**1/2 cup chopped zucchini**

**1/2 cup chopped green peppers**
**1/2 cup chopped onions**
**1/2 cup chopped fresh broccoli florets**

## Directions:

1. Preheat oven to 375 degrees.
2. Roll out crescent rolls to fit a large non-stick cookie sheet.
3. Bake approximately 12 minutes. Take out when brown and let it cool.
4. While the crust is cooling, mix the softened cream cheese with the ranch dressing.
5. Cut up washed vegetables and combine with cream cheese mixture.
6. When the crust is cooled, spread the cream cheese mixture on top.
7. Cool in refrigerator for at least 30 minutes before eating.
8. Cut into squares.

**Nutritional information per serving (daily value):** Calories 417; Protein 10g (21%); Total Fat 27g (41%) (Sat. 12g (61%)); Chol. 66mg (22%); Carb. 36g (12%); Fiber 2g (9%); Sugars 7g; Calcium 171mg (1%); Iron 3mg (14%); Sodium 543mg (23%); Vit. C 30mg (50%); Vit. A 929 IU (19%); Trans fat .02g

# Veggie and Cream Cheese Roll-Ups

| Category: Midday Gourmet | Prep and Cook Time: 15 minutes | Serves: 4 |
|---|---|---|

| Food Cost (per serving) | Restaurant Price | 1 Month Savings | 1 Year Savings |
|---|---|---|---|
| $1.50 | $4.50 | $12.00 | $144.00 |

This is an elegant lunch offering that will be enjoyed by you and your luncheon guest. Cream cheese is relatively high in fat content, but tasty vegetables such as green onion, cilantro, and olives increase the nutritional value of this creative alternative to a sandwich. This recipe tastes better if you prepare and refrigerate the night before you want to eat it for lunch.

**1/2 bunch green onion, chopped**
**1 small can of olives, chopped**
**1/2 bunch cilantro, chopped (or substitute parsley)**
**18 oz. cream cheese, softened**
**1/2 cup mild salsa**
**4 large flour or whole-wheat tortillas**

## Directions:

1. Mix first three ingredients with cream cheese.
2. Drain salsa and add to cheese mixture.
3. Spread the mixture on each tortilla.
4. Roll up the tortillas. Put some cream cheese mixture on the end of the tortilla to seal.
5. Store tortillas in a plastic container or foil for at least 7 hours in the refrigerator. Use toothpicks to keep roll-up together.

*Optional:* Add other favorite vegetables.

---

**Nutritional information per serving (daily value):** Calories 320; Protein 6g (4%); Total Fat 25g (38%) (Sat. 12g(4%)); Chol. 62mg (21%); Carb. 20g (7%); Fiber 2g (9%); Sugars 3g; Calcium 126mg (8%); Iron 2mg (13%); Sodium 619mg (26%); Vit. C 3mg (5%);Vit. A 1617 IU (32%); Trans fat 0g

# Quick Hard-Boiled Eggs

| Category: Midday Gourmet | Prep and Cook Time: 45 minutes | Serves: 12 |
|---|---|---|

| Food Cost (per serving) | Restaurant Price | 1 Month Savings | 1 Year Savings |
|---|---|---|---|
| $0.25 | $1.75 | $6.00 | $72.00 |

A single egg with only 72 calories provides 13 essential nutrients in varying amounts, including high-quality protein, choline, folate, iron, and zinc. Have hard-boiled eggs on hand for Grab and Go and for making simple Traditionalist recipes and adding to salads.

**12 eggs**

## Directions:

1. Put 12 eggs in a single layer in a large pot and cover with at least an inch or two of water. Always start with cold water. Set the burner on high and bring the eggs to a boil.
2. As soon as the water boils, remove from the heat (electric stove) for 1 minute. If you have a gas stove, turn down the flame to simmer for 1 minute.
3. After the minute, remove from the heat and cover for 12 minutes.
4. After the 12 minutes, remove the eggs from the pot and put them in very cold or ice water in a mixing bowl.
5. Once the eggs are cooled, place them in a convenient place in the refrigerator.

**Nutritional information per serving (daily value):** Calories 72; Protein 17g (34%); Total Fat 5g (8%) (Sat. 2g (8%)); Chol. 211mg (70%); Carb. .4g (0%); Fiber 0g (0%); Sugars .4g; Calcium 27mg (3%); Iron .9mg (5%); Sodium 70mg (3%); Vit. C 0mg (0%) Vit. A 243 IU (5%); Trans fat 0g

# Banana Raisin Muffins

| Category: Midday Gourmet | Prep and Cook Time: 40 minutes | Serves: 12 |
|---|---|---|

| Food Cost (per serving) | Restaurant Price | 1 Month Savings | 1 Year Savings |
|---|---|---|---|
| $0.50 | $2.00 | $6.00 | $72.00 |

Bananas made their way into the United States in 1876, along with instructions on how to eat them. We've used this potassium-rich food raw in baking ever since. Raisins are also vitamin- and mineral-rich, so this combination in a tasty muffin can be a sweet that is actually good for you. Home-baked are best because you control the fat content. Bakery varieties are often loaded with fat.

**2 cups whole grain toasted oat cereal**
**1-1/4 cups all-purpose flour**
**1/3 cup brown sugar**
**2-1/2 tsp. baking powder**
**1 cup raisins**

**1 egg**
**2/3 cup milk**
**3 tbsp. vegetable oil**
**2–3 mashed bananas**

Preheat oven to 400 degrees.

## Directions:

1. Place paper baking cup liners in a 12-muffin pan.
2. Place cereal in plastic food storage bag, and crush with kitchen tool.
3. In large bowl, mix cereal, flour, brown sugar, and baking powder. Stir in next five ingredients until moistened.
4. Divide batter evenly among muffin cups.
5. Bake 20-23 minutes or until toothpick inserted in center comes out clean and muffins are golden brown.
6. Immediately remove from muffin pan. Can freeze when cooled.

**Nutritional information per serving (daily value):** Calories 149; Protein 2g (5%); Total Fat 5g (7%) (Sat. 0.7 (4%)); Chol. 19mg (6%); Carb. 27g (9%); Fiber 2g (7%); Sugars 18g; Calcium 51mg (5%); Iron 2mg (11%); Sodium 48mg (2%); Vit. C 4mg (7%); Vit. A 206 IU (7%); Trans fat .01g

# Blueberry and Whole-Wheat Muffins

| Category: Midday Gourmet | Prep and Cook Time: 40 minutes | Serves: 12 |
|---|---|---|

| Food Cost (per serving) | Restaurant Price | 1 Month Savings | 1 Year Savings |
|---|---|---|---|
| $0.75 | $2.00 | $5.00 | $60.00 |

Blueberries are a great antioxidant source. Antioxidants reduce cellular inflammation. I have seen similar muffins each costing $2.00 or more in coffee shops or restaurants.

2 tbsp. packed brown sugar
1/4 tsp. ground cinnamon
3/4 cup fat-free milk
1/4 cup canola or soybean oil
1/4 cup honey
1 egg

1 cup all-purpose flour
1 cup whole-wheat flour
3 tsp. baking powder
1/2 tsp. salt
1 cup frozen blueberries DO NOT
    THAW (can also use fresh blueberries)

Preheat oven to 400 degrees.

## Directions:

1. Place paper baking cup liners in a 12-muffin pan.
2. In small bowl, stir together brown sugar and cinnamon, and set aside.
3. In large bowl, beat milk, oil, honey, and egg with spoon until well blended.
4. Stir in flours, baking powder, and salt just until dry ingredients are moistened (batter will be lumpy).
5. Gently mix in blueberries.
6. Divide batter evenly among muffin cups. Sprinkle with sugar-cinnamon topping.
7. Bake 18 to 20 minutes or until toothpick inserted in center comes out clean and muffins are golden brown.
8. Immediately remove from muffin pan. Can freeze when cooled.

**Nutritional information per serving (daily value):** Calories 178; Protein 4g (7%); Total Fat 5g (8%) (Sat. 5g (3%); Chol. 18mg (6%); Carb. 30g (10%); Fiber 1g (4%); Sugars 9g; Calcium 96mg (10%); Iron 1mg (7%); Sodium 136mg (6%); Vit. C 16mg (26%); Vit. A 119 IU (2%); Trans fat 0g

# Trail Mix Snack Bars

| Category: Midday Gourmet | Prep and Cook Time: 25 minutes | Serves: 12 |
|---|---|---|

| Food Cost (per serving) | Restaurant Price | 1 Month Savings | 1 Year Savings |
|---|---|---|---|
| $1.00 approx.* | n/a | n/a | n/a |

It is healthier and cheaper to make your own trail mix snack bars instead of buying them. Trail mix is a concentrated form of energy that is needed when expending large amounts of physical energy as in hiking or running up and down stairs rather than using the elevator.

*Depending on ingredients

**4 cups whole-grain toasted oat cereal**
**3 cups trail mix (seeds, nuts, and dried fruits). Shop where these items are sold in bulk.**
**1/4 cup margarine or butter**

**1 cup packed brown sugar**
**2 tbsp. all-purpose flour**
**1/2 cup corn syrup**
**cooking spray**

## Directions:

1. Use cooking spray on a rimmed cookie sheet.
2. Place cereal in plastic food storage bag and crush with kitchen tool.
3. In large bowl, mix cereal and trail mix, and put on rimmed cookie sheet.
4. In 2-quart saucepan, melt margarine over medium heat; stir in brown sugar, flour, and corn syrup.
5. Cook, stirring occasionally, until mixture comes to a full boil. Boil 1 minute, stirring constantly.
6. Pour mixture evenly over cereal mixture in large bowl or pot; toss to coat.
7. Press mixture into pan. Cool 10 minutes. Cut into 12 snack bars.

**Nutritional information per serving (daily value):** Calories 392; Protein 11g (21%); Total Fat 22g (34%) Sat. 3g (16%)); Chol. 0mg (0%); Carb. 43g (14%); Fiber 4g (17%); Sugars 23g; Calcium 93mg (9%); Iron 5mg (28%); Sodium 131mg (5%); Vit. C 2mg (4%); Vit. A 457 IU (9%); Trans fat 0g

# Social Networker Lunch Style

The Social Networker is someone who likes to organize and enjoys coordinating activities with friends or colleagues.

The recipes in this section outline how a group coordinates a lunch by having each person bring some of the ingredients. When all the ingredients are assembled, a delicious lunch is served. This can be a special lunch for an event such as a birthday or it can be planned as a weekly occurrence.

Another approach for sharing lunches is for five people to work as a team and the person to bring five lunches on his or her designated day. Each person works independently one day a week and the other four he or she enjoys what the other teammates prepare.

Before beginning this Social Networker approach, the team should set some ground rules. An easy one when starting is for each person to bring lunches for everyone from recipes in this book. This establishes that everyone will be spending approximately the same amount of time and money on the individual recipes. As time goes on, expand your recipe choices and by all means be creative. I strongly encourage you to use the recipe websites on page 120.

If you are assigned as the Grab and Go person for your group, go through the list and the easy recipes in the other categories and choose recipes that will supplement the main meal. Buying in larger quantities when you are creating the group lunch may save more money since there will be no expenses for the other four days. Don't forget to add your Grab and Go items in your final lunch cost.

The six recipes in this section are written for a group of five people and list the directions and ingredients for each person. The cost is calculated for the entire recipe and not for individual people. In all six recipes, one person brings Grab and Go items, Creative Lunch salad, or Midday Gourmet salads or soup to round out the lunch. The organizer can easily modify group and recipe proportions. Each person spends approximately 15 minutes preparing his or her part of the meal.

# Social Networker Group Recipes

# Vegetarian Taco Salad

| Category: Social Networker | Prep and Cook Time: 15 min/person | Serves: 5 |
|---|---|---|

| Food Cost (per serving) | Restaurant Price | 1 Month Savings | 1 Year Savings |
|---|---|---|---|
| $3.00 | $7.00 | $16.00 | $192.00 |

This is a wonderful way to share lunch. Be creative and include favorite ingredients such as cooked chicken or ground beef for the meat lovers.

**1 head lettuce, torn in small pieces**
**2 tomatoes, chopped**
**1 medium onion, chopped**
**1 (5–6 oz.) can of black olives, chopped**
**1 or 2 (15 oz.) cans of kidney beans, drained**
**8 oz. Cheddar cheese, grated**
**1 (10 oz.) pkg. corn chips**

**8 oz. salsa (mild, medium, or hot depending on the group preference)**
**pkg. 10 flour or whole-wheat tortillas**
**1 small container sour cream *(optional)***

**If you want to add meat, have someone bring cooked chicken cut in small pieces or cooked ground beef.**

## Directions:

Person 1  Cut up lettuce, tomatoes, and onion.
Person 2  Cut up olives; heat cooked kidney beans and grate cheese.
Person 3  Bring corn chips and a jar of salsa.
Person 4  Bring tortillas and sour cream.
Person 5  Bring Grab and Go items or a Midday Gourmet soup or an assortment of fruits.

**30 Minutes before Lunch:**
Arrange food in separate bowls, heat tortillas if possible, grab a plate, and create your own taco salad.

**Nutritional information per serving (daily value):** Calories 491; Protein 14g (28%); Total Fat 30g (45%) Sat. 10g (50%); Chol. 37mg (12%); Carb. 48g (10%); Fiber 6g (24%); Sugars 4g; Calcium 382mg (38%); Iron 4mg (21%); Sodium 141mg (48%); Vit. C 16mg (27%); Vit. A 4330 IU (87%); Trans fat 0.22g

# Pasta Salad with Cheese and Black Beans

| Category: | Social Networker | | Prep and Cook Time: | 15 min/person | Serves: | 5 |
|---|---|---|---|---|---|---|

| Food Cost (per serving) | Restaurant Price | 1 Month Savings | 1 Year Savings |
|---|---|---|---|
| $2.00 | $7.00 | $20.00 | $240.00 |

Black beans and cheese turn a pasta salad into a high-protein, hearty meal. This dish is an excellent social network offering that will please many palates.

**6 oz. penne pasta, cooked to package directions**
**1 (16 oz.) jar salsa (mild, medium, hot, according to group preferences**
**1 (15 oz.) can black beans, rinsed and drained**
**1 cup shredded Jack, Cheddar, or Feta cheese**
**1/4 cup green peppers, chopped**
**1/4 cup onion, sliced thin**
**salt and pepper, to taste**

## Directions:

Person 1    Cook pasta the night before, and refrigerate.
Person 2    Combine jar of salsa and drained black beans.
Person 3    Grate or bring shredded cheese.
Person 4    Cut up green pepper and onion.
Person 5    Bring Grab and Go items, Midday Gourmet soup, or fruit and rolls.

**30 Minutes before Lunch:**
Combine all the ingredients in a large bowl with lid, mix, and refrigerate. Can use plastic or aluminum foil to cover bowl for refrigeration.

---

**Nutritional information per serving (daily value):** Calories 159; Protein 7g (14%); Total Fat 5g (7%) (Sat. 3g (14%)); Chol. 13mg (4%); Carb. 22g (7%); Fiber 1g (4%); Sugars 1g; Calcium 113mg (11%); Iron 0.49mg (3%); Sodium 78mg (3%); Vit. C 4mg (7%);  Vit. A 126 IU (3%); Trans fat 0g

# Cobb Salad

| Category: | Social Networker | Prep and Cook Time: | 15 min/person | Serves: | 5 |
|-----------|------------------|---------------------|---------------|---------|---|

| Food Cost (per serving) | Restaurant Price | 1 Month Savings | 1 Year Savings |
|-------------------------|------------------|-----------------|----------------|
| $2.50 | $8.50 | $24.00 | $288.00 |

This salad is chock full of vitamins and minerals, and chicken and eggs are an excellent source of protein. Cobb Salad is pricey if purchased in a restaurant but economical if prepared at home.

**1 head romaine lettuce**
**1 head Boston or red leaf lettuce**
**1 pkg. sliced bacon (turkey bacon works fine)**
**2 ripe avocados, peeled and cut in small pieces**
**2 hard-boiled eggs, finely chopped**
**2 tomatoes, chopped**
**2 whole skinless, boneless cooked breasts or 1 cup of cooked chicken**

**Homemade Salad Dressing**
  **2/3 cup red wine vinegar**
  **2 tbsp. Dijon mustard**
  **1 cup olive oil**
  **1 cup finely grated blue cheese (can substitute Roquefort)**
  **2 tsp. sugar**
  **salt and pepper, to taste.**
  **Mix ingredients in jar with lid and shake rigorously.**

**Nutritional information per serving (daily value):** Calories 263; Protein 13g (26%); Total Fat 13g (20%) (Sat. 6g (29%)); Chol. 25mg (8%); Carb. 24g (8%); Fiber 4g (15%); Sugars 3g; Calcium 279mg (28%); Iron 2mg (12%); Sodium 371mg (15%); Vit. C 12mg (20%); Vit. A 2523 IU (50%); Trans fat 0g

## Directions:

Person 1   Cut up lettuce, tomatoes, and avocados.

Person 2   Cook and drain bacon the night before. When cooled, break into small pieces. Hard-boil eggs, and cut up.

Person 3   Cook or purchase 1 cup of cooked chicken the night before. When cooled, cut up in small pieces.

Person 4   Make the salad dressing the night before, and refrigerate or purchase 1 bottle of blue cheese or Roquefort salad dressing and refrigerate. Bring large serving plate and arrange ingredients on top of the lettuce in rows. Combining ingredients also works.

Person 5   Bring Grab and Go items, Midday Gourmet soup or fruit and rolls.

**30 Minutes before Lunch:**
Layer lettuce on serving plate and arrange other ingredients in rows. Ingredients can be combined, but if there are vegetarians in the group, separate the chicken and bacon. Keep dressing on the side.

# Tuna Baguette Sandwiches

| Category: Social Networker | Prep and Cook Time: 15 min/person | Serves: 5 |
|---|---|---|

| Food Cost (per serving) | Restaurant Price | 1 Month Savings | 1 Year Savings |
|---|---|---|---|
| $2.50 | $6.50 | $16.00 | $192.00 |

This sandwich is an interesting combination of vegetables and tuna providing half the daily amount of protein. It's easy to convert this recipe to meat, cheese, and vegetable sub-sandwiches.

**5 9-inch baguette bread rolls**
**5 tbsp. olive oil**
**3 cans chunk light tuna in water**
**1-1/2 cup mayonnaise**
**2 cloves of garlic, chopped fine**

**1/4 onion, thinly sliced**
**2 tomatoes, sliced**
**2 cucumbers, sliced**
**2 cans olives, chopped**
**10 fresh basil leaves or cilantro**

## Directions:

Person 1  Slice the loaves of bread in half length-wise, hollow out the bread, and spread olive oil on both sides of the opened crust. Place in plastic wrap.

Person 2  In a small bowl, mix the drained tuna fish, mayonnaise, onion, and garlic.

Person 3  Slice tomatoes and cucumbers.

Person 4  Cut up olives, and wash and cut basil or cilantro.

Person 5  Grab and Go items, Creative Lunch salad, or Midday Gourmet soup.

**30 Minutes before Lunch**

1. Layer all the ingredients on the hollow baguette rolls.
2. Put each filled sandwich back in plastic wrap. Press the sandwich by putting a cookie sheet and some cans on top for weight; leave it there for 15 minutes.

**Nutritional information per serving (daily value):** Calories 690; Protein 53g (106%); Total Fat 30g (48%) (Sat. 5g (23%)); Chol. 18mg (6%); Carb. 57g (19%); Fiber 11g (45%); Sugar 6g; Calcium 900mg (90%); Iron 20mg (111%); Sodium 1193mg (50%); Vit. C 91mg (152%); Vit. A 24427 IU (489%); Trans fat 0g

# Meat and Cheese Platter/Sandwiches

| Category: | Social Networker | Prep and Cook Time: | 15 min/person | Serves: | 5 |
|---|---|---|---|---|---|

| Food Cost (per serving) | Restaurant Price | 1 Month Savings | 1 Year Savings |
|---|---|---|---|
| $3.00 | $7.00 | $16.00 | $192.00 |

Meat and cheese provide high energy and protein. Add some vegetables and fruit to round out this luncheon selection.

**1-1/2 lbs. thinly sliced ham or a variety of lunchmeats**
**1-1/2 lbs. thinly sliced Cheddar cheese or variety of cheeses**
**10 slices bread or rolls**
**1 tbsp. butter**
**3/4 cup mayonnaise**
**1/2 cup mustard**
**1/2 head lettuce separated into leaves**
**3 Roma tomatoes, thinly sliced**

## Directions:

Person 1    1/2 lb. of meat and butter or margarine.

Person 2    1/2 lb. of meat and mayonnaise.

Person 3    1/2 lb. of meat and mustard.

Person 4    1-1/2 lb. of sliced cheese, and bread or rolls

Person 5    Lettuce and tomatoes cut up and Grab and Go items.

**30 Minutes before Lunch**

1. Place lettuce on platter, and put meat, cheese and tomatoes on top.
2. Place condiments in separate bowls next to platter.
3. Cover and refrigerate the meat and cheese platter.

**Nutritional information per serving (daily value):** Calories 752; Protein 42g (84%); Total Fat 53g (82%) (Sat. 22g (111%)); Chol. 146mg (49%); Carb. 27g (9%); Fiber 1g (6%); Sugars 2g; Calcium 642mg (64%); Iron 3mg (17%); Sodium 2150mg (90%); Vit. C .31mg (1%); Vit. A 922IU (18%); Trans fat 0.003g

# Fresh Fruit Platter with Yogurt

| Category: Social Networker | | Prep and Cook Time: 15 min/person | Serves: 2 |
|---|---|---|---|

| Food Cost (per serving)* | Restaurant Price | 1 Month Savings | 1 Year Savings |
|---|---|---|---|
| $3.00 | $7.00 | $16.00 | $192.00 |

Fresh fruit is always a welcome and nutritional selection for lunch. The fruit listed below gives you a nice variety, but feel free to choose the fresh fruits you like and watch the sales. This is always a favorite for folks of all ages.

1/2 head lettuce
1/2 large ripe melon or 1 small melon
1/2 ripe pineapple
1 lb. grapes
1 lb. strawberries

2 bananas
1-1/2 lbs. thinly sliced cheddar
    cheese or variety of cheeses
2 cups plain yogurt

*In-season fruit prices

## Directions:

Person 1   Cut up 1/2 head of lettuce and melon in small pieces.
Person 2   Cut up 1/2 pineapple and 1 lb. of grapes. For cutting instructions, go to youtube.com.
Person 3   Cut up strawberries and bananas in small pieces.
Person 4   Bring a 16 oz. container of yogurt and a spoon.
Person 5   Bring rolls and a Grab and Go item.

**30 Minutes before Lunch**

1. Place lettuce on large dish or platter, and place cut-up fruit on top.
2. Place yogurt in a bowl next to the platter.
3. Cover and refrigerate until lunchtime.
4. Serve with rolls and Grab and Go item.

**Nutritional information per serving (daily value):** Calories 262; Protein 7g (13%); Total Fat 4g (6%) (Sat. 2g (11%)); Chol. 13mg (4%); Carb. 59g (19%); Fiber 6g (24%); Sugars 42g; Calcium 174mg (17%); Iron 2mg (9%); Sodium 68mg (3%); Vit. C 137mg (228%), Vit. A 4782 IU (96%); Trans fat 0g

# Resources

# Monthly Calendar

| Sun | Mon | Tues | Wed | Thu | Fri | Sat |
|---|---|---|---|---|---|---|
| **Date:**<br><br>Price:<br><br>Savings: | **Date:**<br><br>Price:<br><br>Savings: | **Date:**<br><br>Price:<br><br>Savings: | **Date:**<br><br>Price:<br><br>Savings: | **Date:**<br><br>Price:<br><br>Savings: | **Date:**<br><br>Price:<br><br>Savings: | **Date:**<br><br>Price:<br><br>Savings: |
| **Date:**<br><br>Price:<br><br>Savings: | **Date:**<br><br>Price:<br><br>Savings: | **Date:**<br><br>Price:<br><br>Savings: | **Date:**<br><br>Price:<br><br>Savings: | **Date:**<br><br>Price:<br><br>Savings: | **Date:**<br><br>Price:<br><br>Savings: | **Date:**<br><br>Price:<br><br>Savings: |
| **Date:**<br><br>Price:<br><br>Savings: | **Date:**<br><br>Price:<br><br>Savings: | **Date:**<br><br>Price:<br><br>Savings: | **Date:**<br><br>Price:<br><br>Savings: | **Date:**<br><br>Price:<br><br>Savings: | **Date:**<br><br>Price:<br><br>Savings: | **Date:**<br><br>Price:<br><br>Savings: |
| **Date:**<br><br>Price:<br><br>Savings: | **Date:**<br><br>Price:<br><br>Savings: | **Date:**<br><br>Price:<br><br>Savings: | **Date:**<br><br>Price:<br><br>Savings: | **Date:**<br><br>Price:<br><br>Savings: | **Date:**<br><br>Price:<br><br>Savings: | **Date:**<br><br>Price:<br><br>Savings: |

# Shopping List for _____
DATE

| **Produce** (fresh fruits and vegetables) | **Dairy** (refrigerated milk, eggs, cheese, etc) |
|---|---|
| **Dry Food** (cereal, rice, pasta, sugar, etc.) | **Canned Goods** (salad dressing, barbeque, pasta sauce) |
| **Frozen Food** | **Meats, Tofu, Grains, Nuts** |
| **Grab and Go Items** | **Kitchen Supplies** (tools, lunch bags, sandwich bags, wrappings) |
| **Other** (snacks, drinks, etc.) | **Other** (snacks, drinks, etc.) |

*What Are You Doing For Lunch?* © 2011 Mona Meighan

# Grab and Go List

Check the foods you plan to buy and add them to your weekly shopping list. Then list them on your monthly calendar. Depending on your time and appetite, take the number of items that is right for you. I have found that three items are my own good number, but don't forget snack times.

**Refrigerator/Freezer**
- ☐ Hard-boiled eggs
- ☐ Healthy frozen entrées
- ☐ Hummus, pesto, guacamole, cream cheese, or peanut butter for dipping vegetables or spreading on crackers and bread
- ☐ Leftovers
- ☐ Pickles
- ☐ Yogurt (plain is healthiest)
- ☐ Other

**Fruits**
- ☐ Apples
- ☐ Bananas
- ☐ Berries
- ☐ Grapes
- ☐ Pears
- ☐ Other

**Vegetables**
- ☐ Broccoli
- ☐ Carrots
- ☐ Cauliflower
- ☐ Celery
- ☐ Cucumbers
- ☐ Greens (Dressing)
- ☐ Peppers
- ☐ Sprouts
- ☐ Snap peas
- ☐ Tomatoes
- ☐ Zucchini
- ☐ Other

**Pantry**
- ☐ Almonds, cashews, sunflower seeds
- ☐ Chips
- ☐ Crackers
- ☐ Dark chocolate bars
- ☐ Fruit leather, raisins, dried cranberries
- ☐ Healthy muffins
- ☐ Peanut butter
- ☐ Non-sweetened fruit packages
- ☐ Trail mix granola
- ☐ Other

**Drinks**
- ☐ Juices
- ☐ Water
- ☐ Other

**Spreads**
- ☐ Cream cheese
- ☐ Hummus
- ☐ Pesto
- ☐ Other

# Recipes at a Glance

| Recipe | Page | Category | Food Cost | Savings* | Economical** | Vegetarian |
|---|---|---|---|---|---|---|
| Hummus Salad Wrap | 21 | Almost Grab and Go | $1.00 | $4.00 | Y | Y |
| Fresh Basil and Tomato Sandwich | 22 | Almost Grab and Go | $1.00 | $4.00 | Y | Y |
| Pesto and Tomato Sandwich | 23 | Almost Grab and Go | $1.50 | $3.50 | Y | Y |
| Peanut Butter and Banana Wrap | 24 | Almost Grab and Go | $1.00 | $3.50 | Y | Y |
| Peanut Butter, Apple, and Granola Wrap | 25 | Almost Grab and Go | $1.00 | $3.50 | Y | Y |
| Peanut Butter and Jelly Sandwich | 26 | Almost Grab and Go | $0.50 | $2.50 | Y | Y |
| Strawberries and Cream Cheese Sandwich | 27 | Almost Grab and Go | $1.00 | $3.50 | Y | Y |
| Cream Cheese and Jelly Sandwich | 28 | Almost Grab and Go | $0.50 | $2.50 | Y | Y |

*Savings refers to how much you can save by ordering the same or similar item in a sit-down restaurant including the tip.

**Economical is a cost of $2.50 or less. Even if inflation raises the prices of food, the ratio will probably remain the same.

| Recipe | Page | Category | Food Cost | Savings* | Economical** | Vegetarian |
|---|---|---|---|---|---|---|
| Cucumbers and Cream Cheese Sandwich | 29 | Almost Grab and Go | $1.00 | $3.00 | Y | Y |
| 5-Minute Egg Salad Sandwich | 33 | Traditionalist | $1.00 | $4.00 | Y | Y |
| Curried Egg Salad Sandwich | 34 | Traditionalist | $1.00 | $4.00 | Y | Y |
| Egg Salad with Apples and Almonds | 35 | Traditionalist | $1.50 | $4.00 | Y | Y |
| Ham and Cheese Wrap | 36 | Traditionalist | $3.00 | $4.00 | N | N |
| Pita Bread Meat and Cheese Sandwich | 37 | Traditionalist | $3.00 | $4.00 | N | N |
| Famous Tuna Salad Sandwich | 38 | Traditionalist | $2.00 | $4.00 | Y | N |
| Tuna Parmesan Sandwich | 39 | Traditionalist | $2.00 | $4.00 | Y | N |
| Tuna Apple Sandwich | 40 | Traditionalist | $2.50 | $4.00 | Y | N |
| Shrimp Salad Sandwich | 45 | Creative Lunch | $4.00 | $3.50 | N | N |

*Savings refers to how much you can save by ordering the same or similar item in a sit-down restaurant including the tip.

**Economical is a cost of $2.50 or less. Even if inflation raises the prices of food, the ratio will probably remain the same.

| Recipe | Page | Category | Food Cost | Savings* | Economical** | Vegetarian |
|---|---|---|---|---|---|---|
| Curried Chicken Salad | 46 | Creative Lunch | $3.00 | $4.50 | N | N |
| Grandma's Chicken Salad Sandwich | 47 | Creative Lunch | $3.50 | $4.00 | N | N |
| Chicken/ Turkey Caesar Wrap | 48 | Creative Lunch | $1.50 | $5.50 | Y | N |
| Provolone-Pesto Wrap | 49 | Creative Lunch | $2.50 | $4.50 | Y | Y |
| Basil, Tomato, and Mozzarella Cheese Salad | 50 | Creative Lunch | $1.50 | $4.00 | Y | Y |
| Smoked Salmon and Greens | 51 | Creative Lunch | $2.50 | $5.50 | Y | N |
| Tuna Avocado Salad | 52 | Creative Lunch | $2.00 | $5.50 | Y | N |
| Spinach Salad with Feta and Walnuts | 53 | Creative Lunch | $2.00 | $5.50 | Y | Y |
| Strawberry/ Mango Salad | 54 | Creative Lunch | $2.00 | $6.00 | Y | Y |
| Classic Caesar Salad | 55 | Creative Lunch | $2.50 | $5.00 | Y | Y |
| Mixed Green Salad | 56 | Creative Lunch | $1.50 | $4.50 | Y | Y |

*Savings refers to how much you can save by ordering the same or similar item in a sit-down restaurant including the tip.

**Economical is a cost of $2.50 or less. Even if inflation raises the prices of food, the ratio will probably remain the same.

| Recipe | Page | Category | Food Cost | Savings* | Economical** | Vegetarian |
|--------|------|----------|-----------|----------|--------------|------------|
| Fruit and Nut Salad | 57 | Creative Lunch | $2.00 | $5.50 | Y | Y |
| Black Bean and Corn Salad | 58 | Creative Lunch | $1.00 | $5.00 | Y | Y |
| Mango Smoothie | 59 | Creative Lunch | $2.00 | $3.00 | Y | Y |
| Fruit and Greens Smoothie | 60 | Creative Lunch | $1.50 | $2.50 | Y | Y |
| Fruit and Vegetable Smoothie | 61 | Creative Lunch | $1.50 | $2.50 | Y | Y |
| Pear and Kale Smoothie | 62 | Creative Lunch | $1.50 | $2.50 | Y | Y |
| Yogurt Parfait | 63 | Creative Lunch | $2.00 | $3.50 | Y | Y |
| Homemade Vegetable Stew | 69 | Midday Gourmet | $1.50 | $6.50 | Y | Y |
| Easy Spinach Lasagna | 70 | Midday Gourmet | $1.50 | $7.00 | Y | Y |
| Cooking a Whole Chicken | 71 | Midday Gourmet | $1.50 | $6.00 | Y | N |
| Homemade Chili | 72 | Midday Gourmet | $2.00 | $4.50 | Y | N |
| Homemade Vegetarian Chili | 73 | Midday Gourmet | $1.50 | $4.00 | Y | Y |

*Savings refers to how much you can save by ordering the same or similar item in a sit-down restaurant including the tip.

**Economical is a cost of $2.50 or less. Even if inflation raises the prices of food, the ratio will probably remain the same.

| Recipe | Page | Category | Food Cost | Savings* | Economical** | Vegetarian |
|--------|------|----------|-----------|----------|--------------|------------|
| Homemade Meatballs | 74 | Midday Gourmet | $1.00 | $4.50 | Y | N |
| Beef and Tomato Stew | 75 | Midday Gourmet | $2.50 | $5.50 | Y | N |
| Roast Beef for Sandwiches | 76 | Midday Gourmet | $2.50 | $5.50 | Y | N |
| 15-Minute Hummus | 77 | Midday Gourmet | $0.50 | $2.00 | Y | Y |
| 15-Minute Pesto | 78 | Midday Gourmet | $1.00 | $1.50 | Y | Y |
| Grandma's Chicken Soup | 79 | Midday Gourmet | $2.00 | $4.00 | Y | N |
| Fresh Vegetable Soup | 80 | Midday Gourmet | $1.00 | $4.00 | Y | Y |
| Tomato and Basil Soup | 81 | Midday Gourmet | $1.50 | $4.00 | Y | Y |
| Chicken Tortilla Soup | 82 | Midday Gourmet | $2.50 | $4.50 | Y | N |
| Vegetarian Corn Chowder | 83 | Midday Gourmet | $1.50 | $3.00 | Y | Y |
| Vegetarian Minestrone Soup | 84 | Midday Gourmet | $1.50 | $4.50 | Y | Y |
| Fresh Carrot Soup | 85 | Midday Gourmet | $1.00 | $3.50 | Y | Y |

*Savings refers to how much you can save by ordering the same or similar item in a sit-down restaurant including the tip.

**Economical is a cost of $2.50 or less. Even if inflation raises the prices of food, the ratio will probably remain the same.

| Recipe | Page | Category | Food Cost | Savings* | Economical** | Vegetarian |
|---|---|---|---|---|---|---|
| Fresh Salmon and Spinach Salad | 86 | Midday Gourmet | $3.50 | $5.00 | N | N |
| Pasta Salad with Black Beans and Spinach | 87 | Midday Gourmet | $1.50 | $6.00 | Y | Y |
| Fresh Fruit Salad | 88 | Midday Gourmet | $2.00 | $5.00 | Y | Y |
| Greek Tofu Salad | 89 | Midday Gourmet | $2.00 | $5.00 | Y | Y |
| Eggplant Parmesan Sandwich | 90 | Midday Gourmet | $2.00 | $3.50 | Y | Y |
| Ham, Cheese, and Asparagus Sandwich | 91 | Midday Gourmet | $3.50 | $4.00 | N | N |
| Veggie Cream Cheese Squares | 92 | Midday Gourmet | $2.00 | $3.00 | Y | Y |
| Veggie and Cream Cheese Roll-Ups | 93 | Midday Gourmet | $1.50 | $3.00 | Y | Y |
| Quick Hard-Boiled Eggs | 94 | Midday Gourmet | $0.25 | $1.50 | Y | Y |
| Banana Raisin Muffins | 95 | Midday Gourmet | $0.50 each | $1.50 | Y | Y |

*Savings refers to how much you can save by ordering the same or similar item in a sit-down restaurant including the tip.

**Economical is a cost of $2.50 or less. Even if inflation raises the prices of food, the ratio will probably remain the same.

| Recipe | Page | Category | Food Cost | Savings* | Economical** | Vegetarian |
|---|---|---|---|---|---|---|
| Blueberry and Whole-Wheat Muffins | 96 | Midday Gourmet | $0.75 each | $1.25 | Y | Y |
| Trail Mix Snack Bars | 97 | Midday Gourmet | $1.00 | N/A*** | Y | Y |
| Vegetarian Taco Salad | 101 | Social Networker | $3.00 | $4.00 | N | Y |
| Pasta Salad with Cheese and Black Beans | 102 | Social Networker | $2.00 | $5.00 | Y | Y |
| Cobb Salad | 103 | Social Networker | $2.50 | $6.00 | Y | N |
| Tuna Baguette | 105 | Social Networker | $2.50 | $4.00 | Y | N |
| Meat and Cheese Platter/ Sandwiches | 106 | Social Networker | $3.00 | $4.00 | N | N |
| Fresh Fruit Platter with Yogurt | 107 | Social Networker | $3.00 | $4.00 | N | Y |

*Savings refers to how much you can save by ordering the same or similar item in a sit-down restaurant including the tip.

**Economical is a cost of $2.50 or less. Even if inflation raises the prices of food, the ratio will probably remain the same.

*** Depending on ingredients

# Websites to Help With Lunches

## Section 1: Simple Lunch Recipes

When you are ready to expand your list of recipes, try out some of these sites. Let us know the sites you found helpful by sharing them on our blog at www.whatareyoudoingforlunch.com.

1. **The George Mateljan Foundation**, a not-for-profit foundation with no commercial interests or advertising, is a new force for change to help make a healthier you and a healthier world. Recipes and health tips are available. You can get a free subscription to his newsletter, too. Mateljan's recipe page has over 100 quick and easy recipes to try.

   www.whfoods.com/recipestoc.php#recipes

2. **Choose your preferred ingredients and find recipes.** This site has a lot of nutritional tips, and offers a step-by-step process to switch to a healthier diet as well as vegan information.

   www.nutritionmd.org/recipes/index.html

3. **These two websites offer a large assortment of easy-to-prepare recipes including lunches.**

   www.Allrecipes.com

   www.not-just-recipes.com/Vegetarian-Lunch-Recipes.html
   Vegetarian lunch ideas

4. **The journey of a frugal mom going organic and many more lunch ideas blog.**

   www.lunchboxlimbo.blogspot.com

5. **Bento box ideas with your Grab and Go item.**

   www.youtube.com/watch?v=8XO4Vag9zsY

**6.** **Easy lunch ideas especially if you are a Bento Box fan.**

www.easylunchboxes.smugmug.com

www.laptoplunches.com

## Section 2: Handy Lunch Products

**7.** **Why use recyclable lunch products?** Read about what we are doing to our environment at lunchtime.

www.worldcentric.org

**8.** **Non-toxic, no BPA plastic containers with compartments.**

www.easylunchboxes.com

**9.** **Handy non-plastic food containers and more.**

www.reuseit.com

**10.** **Stainless steel containers with dividers that are eco-friendly.**

www.lunchbots.com

**11.** **This site has all types of lunch bags to substitute for the traditional brown bag.** Accessories to bring with lunch are also available.

www.containerstore.com

**12.** **If you want a complete list of kitchen tools and pantry essentials, check out this site.**

www.whatscookingamerica.com

**13.** **This site includes pantry essentials for setting up a pantry.** Think about your likes and your budget and create the right pantry for you. Your pantry will grow from the recipes you make.

http://whatscookingamerica.net/Q-A/Pantry.htm

**14.** **If you want to share your ideas about organizing a pantry, this site could be very helpful.** Included on the site is also a sample list of pantry items.

www.wikihow.com/Stock-a-Kitchen-Pantry

## Section 3: Research and News about Lunches

**15.** **This article emphasizes the difference between a good and bad lunch and that all good lunches do not have to be from a restaurant.** This site is a must for those who eat at their desks or spend their lunch hour at meetings.

http://taddgiles.com/posts/lunch-is-important

**16.** **This site supports brown bagging to save money, to control what you are eating, and to eat healthier.** The lunch bots, an alternative to the traditional lunch container, is referenced.

www.wellsphere.com    *Search:* healthy lunches

**17.** **Great resource for the college student in all of us offering tips and recipes for lunches.**

www.jhsph.edu/student_affairs/Lunch

**18.** **If you are interested in improving and reforming school lunches**, go to this site and join the campaign sponsored by the Physicians Committee for Responsible Medicine (PCRM).

www.healthyschoollunches.org

**19.** **This site offers a Shoppers Guide to Pesticides**. When you are shopping, carry this handy guide that shows what fruits and vegetables are high in pesticide residues. I recommend buying organic for those on the high pesticide list.

www.ewg.org/foodnews

# Authors

www.whatareyoudoingforlunch.com

Mona Meighan has a doctorate in Education and has taught classes and developed curricula for adults and children for the past 35 years. She became aware that many people, including herself, ignore lunch by skipping it entirely, eating junk food in place of lunch, or spending too much money purchasing lunches from restaurants. When her son suddenly died at the age of 26 from undiagnosed diabetes, resolving the lunch dilemma became her personal focus. Mona wrote this book as a guide to help others develop healthier habits for lunchtime and to help answer the question "What Are You Doing for Lunch?" without the guesswork of figuring out where to start. A portion of the proceeds from the book are donated to non-profit organizations in honor of her son to support enlightened awareness of providing healthy, economical lunches.

dehart.ss@frontier.com

Sara S. DeHart has a doctorate in Developmental Psychology and a graduate degree Public Health Nursing. Since retirement from academic nursing she has focused on writing and is a strong advocate for self-care solutions for many of the medical problems that Americans now face. She believes that a healthy diet and nutrition are gateways to health and one solution to our national health crisis of obesity in children and young adults. She has served as a Visiting Scholar at the University of Washington, School of Nursing in Seattle. She currently lives in the Northwest and writes about Public Health and Public Policy.

# Index

# Index of Recipes